Praise for

A HAPPY MOVE

"*A Happy Move* heals lives and bodies when you let your heart make up your mind. I have learned this from people who induce self-healing through change in their lives. Let Devra Jacobs's experience and wisdom guide you to learn how to make your happy move and heal your life too."

—**Bernie Siegel, MD,**
author of *Love, Medicine & Miracles*

"Devra Jacobs is the authority on moving! When you have to make a move, this book, *A Happy Move*, will show you how to not make expensive mistakes. The authors guide you through all of the proper planning from start to finish without wasting your time or money. Simple to follow, it even includes access to videos to avoid expensive replacements of broken items."

—**Dr. Anthony M. Criniti IV (aka Dr. Finance®),**
leading financial scientist and author of
bestseller *The Survival of the Richest*

Everything You Need to Know
Before and After the Boxes
Are Packed

A HAPPY MOVE

Devra Jacobs *and* **Brit Elders**

BEYOND WORDS
Portland, Oregon

BEYOND WORDS

1750 S.W. Skyline Blvd., Suite 20
Portland, Oregon 97221-2543
503-531-8700 / 503-531-8773 fax
www.beyondword.com

First Beyond Words paperback edition March 2024

BEYOND WORDS PUBLISHING and colophon are registered trademarks of Beyond Words Publishing. Beyond Words is an imprint of Simon & Schuster, LLC

For more information about special discounts for bulk purchases, please contact Beyond Words Special Sales at 503-531-8700 or specialsales@beyondword.com.

Managing editor: Lindsay Easterbrooks-Brown
Editors: Michele Ashtiani Cohn and Bailey Potter
Copyeditor: Ashley Van Winkle
Proofreader: Kristin Thiel
Design: Devon Smith
Composition: William H. Brunson Typography Services

Manufactured in China

10 9 8 7 6 5 4 3 2 1

Library of Congress Control Number: 2023036373

The corporate mission of Beyond Words Publishing, Inc.: *Inspire to Integrity*

For my daughter, Rebecca Stinson, who, without question, would pack a box and go anywhere anytime. And for my granddaughter, Alora Stinson, who convinced us to finally stop moving and stay put.

—Devra Jacobs

Contents

Foreword

by Dr. Donna Marks

When I think of moving, chaos enters my mind. Everyone is uptight and disoriented. The house looks like King Kong shook it until everything landed helter-skelter. Belongings are shoved into a moving vehicle, and when they reach their destination, things are broken or I endlessly look for missing items. Then, it can take weeks or months to set up bank and utility accounts, find new physicians, and get acclimated. The authors of this book provide numerous examples of lessons learned during chaotic moves and their takeaways from those experiences. Devra, having moved twenty-nine times in forty years, does a stellar job of turning all her moving mistakes into a miracle of helping others avoid the same pitfalls. When you're prepared, you're also more patient, which is key to feeling cool, calm, and collected even amid moving chaos.

After quite a few moves myself, I've learned that pre-planning is key to a calmer—even fun—experience. Stress might be exhilarating for some people, but trust me, when you carefully organize your move, your family will appreciate the lack of drama and bad decisions often made under pressure.

Lists are a great way to avoid stress. I like to have my before, during, and after lists, and *A Happy Move* provides everything I would add to those lists and more. With this book, there's never a reason to be blindsided by having overlooked an important detail.

Whether you're moving next door or across the world, getting *A Happy Move* should be first on your to-do list, and the second thing on that list is to prepare *now*. Procrastinating will turn a molehill into a mountain and make you feel crazy. Careful planning and preparation can create an adventurous experience instead of a living nightmare.

Relocating from one home to another is one of the top stressors in life. Moving to an entirely different region is even more taxing on one's nerves—the farther away from the original location, the harder it is. Everyone, including the family pets, can experience psychological discomfort during a move. Even if there's excitement over the anticipation of something new, the upheaval of relocating and the demands of packing, finding a new home (sometimes sight unseen), and traveling are overwhelming. They can cause anxiety, depression, fighting, and even illness. Yet all these factors can be reduced with sound planning, delegating, and enlisting the family in making it a fun experience.

As soon as you know you might be moving, tell the family so they have time to prepare emotionally. Otherwise, you'll face resentment instead of cooperation. There's nothing worse than rebellious teenagers dragging their feet when you need their help or acting out their frustration instead of talking about it. Sit down with everyone and tell them why you're moving. Ask how they feel about it. Be willing to be flexible about different possibilities. Give everyone a say in the responsibilities. Conversations about what it might be like in the new location, new schools, and how their friends can come visit build cohesion instead of resentment. It's easier to let go of the familiar when there's something exciting to look forward to.

If you like to control things, now is the time to delegate so that you aren't frazzled before you even start packing. This book covers every detail of pre-move, mid-move, and post-move planning to make it as organized as possible. Devra will help you build a team early on by enlisting each family member for specific tasks. For example, teenagers are great at doing online research that can prevent a bad moving experience. Devra tells a story of living in an apartment for two months before learning it was in foreclosure. She thought she'd done her due diligence but learned the hard way to do extra checking when renting on websites. Having teens look up property reviews and investigate locations can give them ownership and take some burdens off parents' shoulders. Even if you're single and solo, enlist friends and relatives to help—it's an excellent opportunity to provide closure and transitional experiences that hold good memories.

When researching and planning for the right location, be sure the area and the climate suit your personality and lifestyle. I wish I'd heard the authors' suggestions about finding a safe neighborhood before one of my moves. I could have avoided living in a dangerous area next to a sex offender. It's hard to pre-plan for the weather and safety because it takes time, and it seems counter-intuitive to spend that time when you have a lot to do. But it's far easier to plan for a safe and comfortable environment before moving than to relocate shortly after you arrive.

Social media can help when seeking new connections or guidance. As a military family, we always lived on the base, which made it easy to make new friends. This was especially helpful when we moved from tropical Florida to arctic Labrador, where we had to stay mostly indoors during the winter. Without friends to share activities in each other's homes, it could have been unnecessarily isolating and depressing.

Packing for your move is a logistical challenge, but one way to minimize stress *before* packing is to declutter. Before I move, I make three piles of stuff: Goodwill, friends, and keeps. Some people like to sell items they no longer want on websites and make a little extra money. Again, teens are great at this and can be highly motivated for a cut of the proceeds.

I also discovered it's often cheaper to buy new furniture instead of paying the movers thousands of dollars moving furniture that was old or wouldn't even work in the new location. I donate the old furniture, get a tax deduction, and then purchase new (or secondhand) for the next home. Another bonus—I can be sure the new furniture will fit in the new home, unlike the time I wound up having a wall-to-wall-sized bed.

I wish I'd read *A Happy Move* before my last move, when the moving company charged by the box. In some cases, they'd filled boxes with wads of paper and very few items, which wound up taking twice as many boxes and costing us twice the quote. One box had three glasses with over twenty sheets of paper wadded around each glass. The worst part was unpacking so many boxes, disassembling them, and then taking them to the recycling center—additional work hours that I desperately needed to spend on getting settled.

After you've decluttered, do an inventory. Don't assume large unboxed items will find their way to their new location. I once moved some things into a warehouse, but when I transferred the items from that location to my home, some of the antiques were missing. When I contacted the company's owner, he ignored my calls and a letter from my attorney. His laissez-faire attitude made it clear that was the last I'd seen of those valuables. If I had taken the time to make a list of items and then checked them off as they were unloaded into the warehouse, I'd still have all my valuables. Better time management on my part would have saved a truckload of stress and financial loss.

A Happy Move provides guidance on choosing a professional moving company, understanding the contract, and avoiding hidden fees. When a close friend of mine was moving, the movers brought all her furniture to the parking lot and only then told her the cost was going to be triple their quote because everything wouldn't fit in the truck (even though they been to her home to assess the cost). She pleaded with them to load as much as possible, but they refused. She had no recourse but to scramble to get a loan from a friend. Carefully reading her contract, looking up reviews, and getting recommendations from friends could have avoided this trauma.

If you're self-moving, plan for extra time and bring plenty of snacks, water, games, pillows, and blankets. One family member can pack the cooler, one might be in charge of entertainment, another can be in charge of pets, and someone else can map out the trip or make hotel reservations. And someone should check the weather conditions so you don't wind up in a hurricane, as Devra did on one of her moves. The key is to let go and allow others to help.

If you're self-moving, make sure you are comfortable driving a large rental truck or trailer. The book provides an entire section on the different kinds of self-moving vehicles as well as the benefits and shortcomings of each. Pre-map your route and stay on course without diverting. Devra gives an example of her app diverting her off the main highway where she wound up on a bad road with a flat tire and nowhere to get assistance.

With the help of this book, whether you're hiring movers or self-moving, the process doesn't have to be difficult. I like to stay in a peaceful state of mind and don't want to be a flustered, frenzied bag of nerves, and this book can help anyone who wants an enjoyable moving experience. But *A Happy Move* isn't just a resource for a better move; its contents help your life be more efficient and organized before, during, and after your relocation.

You don't have to wait until you're unpacked and settled to relax. The best time to have a happy move is to start preparing now.

Introduction

Moving. It's a major life change. It doesn't matter if it's across town or across the country, the notion of moving creates a mixed emotional mindset. A move is anticipated because it's introducing a new avenue of life, but simultaneously, the details that demand your attention can generate an overwhelming sense of dread. There are so many things to take care of before, during, and after a move that the whole event can be daunting. It can be frustrating and, sometimes, even disastrous—or you can make it a successful accomplishment.

The purpose of *A Happy Move* is to help you experience a methodical, functional process that results in a stress-free event. Sprinkled with factual stories and firsthand experiences that illustrate potential pitfalls, this book is your moving owner's manual.

Though this book is for everyone, keep in mind that the methods and circumstances of any move will be different. Moving to a rented apartment in the city can't be equated to moving to a home in a rural area. Every possible moving situation will be different based on what is available in that area as well as what your needs are. Moving is not one-size-fits all, but this book, ideally, is!

Lists are provided for you to create and check off the items required to make the process easier, more cost-effective, and more fulfilling. It's a tool for anyone considering a location change, whether it's for work, school, military service, closeness to family and friends, or just a change of scenery. No matter the distance or final destination, you can follow this step-by-step process designed for anyone considering or planning a move.

It's the little things that can make your move a bumpy ride. Of course, most know to contact utility companies to disconnect from services, but did you think to give them your new address so they can send your final bill or refund deposit money? Although deposits are not always required today, many people have lost money because they didn't take that simple step of asking if they had a refund due. Watch for Devra's Tips throughout the book to help you simplify and organize the changes you're facing.

Born out of experience, the method laid out in this book will help alleviate the questions, concerns, and worries of relocating. It can help you avoid schemes, scams, and extra expenses and will serve as your road map for a better moving experience.

A Note from Devra Jacobs

I have moved twenty-nine times in forty years and have hands-on experience that I want to share with you. There are numerous reasons I have moved throughout my life. The first few were simply leaving home, spreading my wings, and getting a job in a location I wanted to be, on my own and away from my family's influence. I was married to a man in the army, which accounted for my moves to Korea, Texas, Alabama, and Florida. Divorce led me to California to be near friends at a time in my life when I needed a support system and the familiarity of an area where I had grown up. As I rebuilt my life as a single mother caring for a young child, I decided I needed the stability of family and moved to Alabama to be close to my parents.

I discovered that I have a wandering spirit and followed it to other parts of the country for the sheer adventure of something new. I have always had a need to follow my wanderlust for new places, foods, and experiences. Some of my moves were born of boredom; I guess I was looking for proverbial greener pastures or maybe a sense of recapturing happier times in my past.

Later in life, as my parents aged, I relocated to be near them to help with injuries and lengthy illnesses. Because of my father's work, they had moved quite a bit too, before eventually settling in central Arizona. Over the years I've moved in and out of Arizona five times.

What made me stop moving were the pleas of my sixteen-year-old granddaughter, who begged her mom and me to stop wandering and let her complete high school and college in the same location. I had dragged the two of them all over the country for years, and she was paying the cost of no real friends or stability. So, I picked Flagstaff, Arizona, where I now live close to my best friend, Brit, in a place of great beauty, wonderful energy, and good schools for my granddaughter.

Will I move again? Probably. But, more than likely, I will stay for some time in this area that I've grown to love and appreciate. And when I move in the future, I will know what works and what doesn't. I will know how to smoothly transition from one location to another, because I've already lived through the snags that will undoubtedly surface.

All my relocation know-how can help you avoid the ups and downs and pitfalls that I have encountered. This book is a resource for you to utilize, learn from, and record all pertinent information for easy access at any time, no matter if you move one time or twenty. It's your hands-on guidebook for moving.

PART 1

BEFORE
YOU MOVE

Chapter 1

Where Will You Call Home?

You've decided to relocate! Maybe it's for business or just to be closer to family. Maybe it's a break from city life or because you're seeking a warmer climate. There are numerous reasons that might precipitate a move, but no matter the incentive, it is a giant undertaking.

Today, people have a wandering spirit; they move on a whim and without a budget. They load the rental truck and head out for a new life adventure. Sometimes they have a plan, sometimes not.

Devra has moved several times not knowing where she would land. Here's one of her experiences:

In one of my moves in the late '90s, I didn't know where I was going to live. I wasn't even sure what town I would settle in. I just blindly drove cross-country with my U-Haul® trailer in tow. I'd decided to take I-40 East and stop when I reached the Atlantic Ocean.

On Memorial Day weekend, I ran out of freeway in Wilmington, North Carolina, and drove down a packed road that led toward the beach and over a bridge to a small island off the coast. I did reach the Atlantic, but beach communities are major summer tourist destinations, especially on holidays. And navigating the traffic and people was almost impossible, not to mention parking my little caravan of two vehicles. I hadn't planned the trip or the timing.

When I finally ran out of road, it took several days to find a place to rent. I was fortunate to find a place that was move-in ready. I hadn't thought about it, but I later realized that I could have been meandering through those small communities for weeks with no place to call home. For almost a week I dragged that U-Haul® to every stop I made. It cost a fortune because I had only rented the truck and tow trailer for three days. Every day was another day of rental fees, which, in the end, almost doubled the original estimate. On top of that, I had also failed to consider the price of gas.

Trying to pull a trailer up and down mountains and across country was exhausting physically, mentally, and financially. The whole adventure was quite an education, and rather ironic, since I thought I would be saving money by doing it all myself instead of hiring professional movers.

It would have been more efficient had I thought about and anticipated all the expenses incurred in that two-thousand-mile move. In hindsight, had I taken the time to research moving options and prepared for a new location, I would have saved myself a lot of money and anxiety.

I have since learned to get at least three estimates, including professional movers, container movers, and rental trucks. I learned to add in the cost of gas, meals, hotels, and miscellaneous expenses that might crop up. Those little details make a big difference in the total cost of the move, and too often they are not considered in the original budget.

There was a wonderful upside to this move: I found a great apartment right on the beach on an island off the coast. But it wasn't long before my wanderlust got the best of me . . . again.

DEVRA'S TIP Know your final destination, get estimates, and consider all expenses for a move. It will save you money and prevent anxiety.

Finding Your Place

It's good to take a minimum of a month to explore where you want to relocate. That gives you time to find a house or apartment and compile information on utilities, schools, and so on. Your research may begin online, but when possible, a reconnaissance trip to your new locale is worth the time and energy. You'll get a feel for the area's schools, shopping, and neighborhoods. If you find a home to purchase or an apartment to lease, you'll probably be able to coordinate the move-in date with the closing date on your old house or the end of the lease on your old apartment.

If you are moving as a family with children, take time to explain to them why you are moving. Listen to their concerns. Their sense of security may be disrupted, and they may feel a sense of loss for the friends and surroundings they're accustomed to. Find things in the new area that will be enticing to them. If they play soccer or baseball or they're on a swim team, locate schools or areas that provide these activities. If they are involved in specific academics, do some research and find what might fit their needs.

A child can feel intimidated when moving to a new school. Investigate the school they will be attending. Sometimes it's wise to speak to a school counselor prior to their enrollment to learn about programs that can help them adjust. Take the time to explain that their friends can still remain part of their lives via any number of means of communication, and assure them that they will make new friends.

Be honest and realistic. Let the children know that all of you will be facing some challenges but that together, you can all have an experience full of growth and adventure.

Know the Area

Moving to an unfamiliar neighborhood can be stressful. Help ease your apprehension by checking crime statistics of the new area online. Some websites will charge a fee, but many help you access the information free of charge. Using SpotCrime.com, you can look at the city and state to get an idea of what types of crimes are most common. AreaVibes.com is free and provides a livability score for the vicinity. Nextdoor.com is a good tool because it's a neighborhood discussion group.

The Dru Sjodin National Sex Offender Public Website (NSOPW. gov) is a public safety resource that accesses sex offender data nation-wide. It's a partnership between the Department of Justice and state and local authorities to help protect adults and children from preda-tors. Most states will allow you to search for sexual predators in your area, but there are a few that do not allow you to search by geographic location. Examples of states that do not file with NSOPW are Ore-gon and Texas. In Oregon, one needs to research the state records of The Oregon State Police Sex Offender Registry Section. In Texas, one would go through the Department of Public Safety to the Texas Public Sex Offender website. These may not list every predator, but they are helpful. Review the resources section at the back of this book for details and more information.

Additional online research can help you know what to expect when you arrive. What is the cost of living in the area you have selected? What are the schools or colleges like? What courses do they offer? Are there hospitals or clinics nearby? How far away is the nearest airport? Is the area prone to severe weather like hurricanes, tornadoes, or flood-ing? What's the usual weather like? Is it hot, cold, or rainy?

Once Devra moved for a job only to discover that she wasn't suited to the climate.

My family had just lived through a horrific hurricane on the East Coast when I received a job offer in Washington State. I jumped at the chance to relocate, and the company offered to pay all moving expenses. It seemed like the timing couldn't be better for a fresh start.

I'd seen the pictures of massive forests and beautiful cities the Northwest is known for, and I looked forward to settling in a new area. The problem was I hadn't done any serious research on the area. I just knew that hurricanes and tornados were not a problem there, and I thought that was good enough for me. But, after six months of almost daily clouds and rain, I found I was experiencing something similar to seasonal affective disorder (SAD). For my own sanity, it was time to move to a more hospitable climate.

DEVRA'S TIP Know what to expect before you arrive at your destination. What is the typical weather throughout the year? Weather is a factor that is often overlooked.

Finding a Place to Live

If you can't make an explorative trip, there are other ways to find a residence. It's generally not recommended that you purchase a home sight unseen or commit to a long-term lease without at least a walk-through of the property. A stopgap motel stay or renting an apartment month-by-month are two options while you look for something more permanent.

Whether during an exploratory trip or a sight-unseen move to a new locale, it's important to provide enough time to find someplace you will be comfortable in and want to call home. Rental markets are volatile, as housing that used to be leased property may now be an Airbnb. Weigh the expenditure of an exploratory trip, including travel, hotel, and meals, versus a prolonged stay in a motel while you search for a new residence after moving. Consider all related costs and how those might affect your budget before making a quick decision.

A motorhome provides an excellent option for investigating a relocation site. You can take your time without the expense of motels and restaurants. Best of all, you can bring the whole family and your pets with you while you look for permanent residence. Motorhomes and camp trailers can be difficult to maneuver in a city, though. You might want to consider towing your own car, parking the RV or trailer at a campsite, and using your vehicle to get around once you're there.

Your Responsibility

When looking for a place to live, it's important to do your due diligence. A little extra time on the computer and phone can save you both money and grief. Regardless of whether you're moving out of state or are staying in state, if you haven't checked the landlord-tenant laws, do so. You should be aware of what laws each party is agreeing to and those laws that vary from state to state. Check the resources at the back of the book for more information.

Property Information Online

Get online and start looking. There are numerous websites that preview homes and apartments, availability, rental terms, locations, and amenities. Reach out to realtors and property managers in your selected area.

If you begin your location search on the internet, verify the information provided on any website. Do a search of the company name plus words like "review," "complaint," or "scam." Follow that up with a check through the local Better Business Bureau (BBB) and Yelp for reviews. Also check with your local secretary of state's website to see if the company is registered to do business in that state. There may be a minimal charge for that secretary of state service, but it's worth it to avoid trouble later.

If you see a website listing, do an online search of the home's address to see if it appears on an actual rental company's website. If it does, it may be what's called a carbon-copy listing, which is a scam. People have jumped at a beautiful picture and a low price, signed papers, paid a deposit, and made the move only to discover that the so-called owner had no right to rent the house or apartment. The unhappy would-be tenants lost their deposit money and had no place to call home.

While the internet is a good way to begin your search, there are certain red flags to be aware of in the process:

- The landlord or rental agents refuse to have a phone conversation and request that everything be done via email.
- The landlord or rental agency refuses to meet with you in person.
- The agency requests money and says they will send the keys once it's been paid.
- The agency requests that you make payment to a company outside the United States.

Unfortunately, these types of scams have become more and more common. It's up to you to be aware of them and to do your due diligence to prevent falling into the trap. Avoid renting or leasing from an owner who registers on an online bulletin board or uses some other form of advertising unless they can prove that they legally own the property.

Devra's experience perfectly illustrates that point:

I'd heard about the scams perpetrated by fake owners on various websites. I decided to be smart and verify the ownership of the condo that I planned to rent. I knew that could be done through the city public records of property ownership. I was sure I had covered my backside with a little bit of research. Boy, was I wrong.

Two months after I had paid to be professionally moved, after I had settled in with my child, pets, and all my belongings, a strange man entered my apartment with a key and demanded I leave everything and vacate the premises immediately. That was how I discovered that the owners had filed for bankruptcy. He informed me that the property had been foreclosed on and was now being managed by a bankruptcy attorney and that I was not legally allowed to be there. After I pleaded my case through tears of panic, he gave me ten days to move out. We lost our deposit of two and a half months' rent and had to find a new home, come up with deposits for the new property, and pay for another company to move us to the new location.

DEVRA'S TIP Verify the details! Your due diligence should include checking online for any court proceedings on the property. That simple step could prevent additional unanticipated expenses and an extra move.

There are some other signals that indicate it might be best to walk away from a listing:

- The online pictures and description of the property or the price seem too good to be true.
- The property is never available for a walk-through.
- Unrealistically low rental prices or little to no upfront deposit.
- Numerous spelling and grammar errors in the rental listing.
- The landlord or rental agency does not request an application or tenant screening.

According to a 2022 article on the Better Business Bureau website, moving scams are becoming a major problem, with more than one thousand complaints filed in 2021.[1] It's always best to see the property and meet the landlord or rental agent before exchanging any money, even before paying the application fee. However, some cities have specific regulations regarding landlord-tenant laws that prohibit the renter from viewing the residence until a deposit has been made. In those cities, when you make a deposit, you're actually paying for the privilege of viewing your potential new residence. Find out if the city or town you are moving to has this type of ordinance. This is just one aspect of due diligence that falls on your shoulders.

And never wire money. If someone tells you that you must wire money before they can proceed, close the door on that property and move in another direction because it's most likely a scam.

Before You Sign

Your research doesn't stop once you think you've found a place that suits your needs. When a potential landlord or rental company doesn't mention running a credit check or fails to request references, a huge yellow caution sign should flash in your mind. This is true especially if they push you to sign the lease or make a deposit. Consider this: it may not be their property to rent or lease, and you might need to dig a little deeper to uncover all the facts. If nothing else, the lack of interest in your habits indicates a landlord that has little or no interest in their property or in you as a tenant.

If you find someplace that looks intriguing, you should check them out through the Better Business Bureau and Yelp or post on local social media groups to ask if anyone knows the area or has had dealings with the management company or landlord you're working through. You might be surprised by the amount of feedback you find.

Subletting: A Word of Caution

Subletting can be very tricky. It involves the property owners and the current tenant, who is leasing to yet another person (you). Typically the owner of the real estate must approve any subletting arrangement, but subletting is subject to any city, county, or state regulations or laws. Always verify what the statutes are and whether or not the original tenant has the right to sublet the place. That may require a review of the original tenant's lease agreement or a discussion with the property owner. Subletting without permission is a very common rental scam in big cities or around college campuses and something to be aware of.

Before you commit to anything or sign a contract of any type, thoroughly read the agreement. You can ask for a copy of the lease document to review. It's probably a warning sign if the landlord balks or refuses to allow you to review the paperwork.

Rental Agencies and Property Management

If you sign with a rental agency or property management company, you should expect to pay an application fee. That fee might include a background check and credit report on you, and every agency or company you sign with will charge a similar fee. Landlord-tenant laws vary from state to state, as do the regulations that govern management companies and real estate agencies. To save money, do your research on the various companies, check online reviews, and interview the rental agents or landlords. If you can, select just one to begin the process with.

If you are dealing with a rental agency or management company, ask for the actual property owner's name and contact information. An agency probably won't comply, but it doesn't hurt to ask. If they refuse to give the owner's name, go through local property ownership records and property tax records. That can often be done online. It's not a necessity, but it is beneficial to have that information available. Not only is it a good way to verify that the owners are up-to-date on their taxes and not in foreclosure, but at some point, you might need to contact the owner if the management company fails to attend to repairs.

Social Media Help

Social media can be a tremendous help when you're trying to find a place to lease or a company to work with on your search. Once you've determined the area you want to settle in, join an online message board such as Facebook or Nextdoor for that specific locale. Ask about properties for lease, reputable property management companies, and realtors who could be of assistance to you. If you have a question about schools, dog parks, shopping malls, or crime rates in the new area, ask. People are usually quite helpful and willing to share their experiences. They can also help you weed out people and companies you might not want to deal with in your before-the-move preparations.

Gather Your References

Moving to any rental property will be easier, and sometimes less costly, if you have references from previous landlords. Try to go back ten years if you can. Landlords look for people who are dependable, pay their rent on time, and don't raise a ruckus.

Ask your previous property owners for letters of reference. They are generally happy to oblige, especially if you give them at least a month's notice of your departure. That's the best time to ask for a letter of recommendation. By giving sufficient notice, you're fulfilling your obligation as a tenant, and that carries weight with the owner.

If possible, do not sign a lease until you or someone you trust has walked through the property. In some locations where rental property is at a premium, the landlord may offer pictures of a comparable apartment at the same location and request a prelease. That means that you sign a lease prior to the current occupant's departure. You are entering into this agreement before ever stepping foot on the property. You will basically know the layout of the place, but you won't know what, if any, damages exist.

If you do sign a prelease on an apartment, verify that any deposit money is refundable if the place is a shambles when you open the door for the first time. If the deposit is not refundable and you have agreed to that, note and photograph every problem and make certain the landlord promptly sees to the repairs.

Watch for Hidden Fees

A common scam reported by renters is that they were quoted a monthly price, but the actual document lists additional fees. In addition to deposits and monthly terms, items like costs and responsibilities of repairs, utilities, trash, homeowners associations (HOA), extra monthly fees for pets, and pool or gym fees can be buried in the fine print. Carefully review the documents and ask questions.

Pets

Pets are part of your family, but many rentals do not allow them. Some properties will accept a cat, a dog, or a bunny but not a reptile or bird. Some will permit one pet but not two, some have weight or breed restrictions, and some may require your pet's vaccination record. Most will require a pet deposit or additional fee of some type. If your pet does no damage to your apartment, other than to your slippers, this deposit is usually refundable. Don't assume this, though. Read the lease or rental agreement to make certain that is the case.

Always be very honest with the landlord about your animals, including how many, what type, the breed, and the gender.

Out Clause in the Lease

What happens when you want to leave this rental? Maybe you're renting short-term while you're in the process of buying a new home, or maybe your job will require that you move. Be certain to include an "out clause" addendum in the lease document that permits you to break the lease for that specific reason.

An out clause is very important if a member of the family is in the military and you're living off the base. It can also apply to roommates, students, and professionals who may have to leave on short notice because of relocation for work.

Don't wait until the last minute to spring this on your landlord or property management company. Be up-front early on in the conversations. They will appreciate it, and it alleviates a potential source of stress for you.

Money

Most landlords will require 1) a cleaning/security deposit, which is usually refundable if you leave the place clean and in good condition when you move out, and 2) the first and last month's rent. Different landlords will define "clean and in good condition" in different ways. Ask your potential landlord what they expect for you to have your cleaning/security deposit refunded.

Some states limit the amount a landlord can require for a security and cleaning deposit. Check with the state's tenant rights to determine the laws about pricing deposits. The resources in the back of the book can help you find your state's landlord-tenant laws.

Quite often, a deposit is required to hold the property, especially in a tight market. In that case, it's best to use a credit card or digital transfer and get a signed receipt that the deposit is for a "hold on the property." Most management companies have deposit agreements available. These will be specific and state that you have made a deposit to hold the property for a specific length of time, the amount of the deposit, and that, should you decline to sign the lease, the deposit will or will not be refunded. If it's nonrefundable, and the time allotted for an inspection is reasonable, discuss an equitable resolution with the management company. They may agree to lower the fee or drop it altogether.

If you are not using a management company or are going through an individual property owner who requires a deposit, create a simple one-page document stating those points. This protects both parties and assures the property owner that you are serious.

You definitely want to request an inside and outside walk-through with the landlord or management company to make certain the rental is livable, clean, well maintained, and insect-free. Take photographs of anything questionable that you find during a walk-through: a dent in a wall, a stain on the carpet, or a door that doesn't close correctly. Make a note in case you need to ask the landlord to clean or repair something. Even if it's a minor issue that doesn't need to be repaired, share the pictures with the landlord to document that the problem was present before you moved in.

Never pay anyone with cash. You can pay a deposit or rent with a cashier's check, check, and sometimes a credit card or via a digital transfer. State clearly on the receipt that the amount is being paid for a specific reason, such as "[dollar amount]—deposit and two months' rent," and list the property address and date of the transaction. Keep your records. Maintain a signed copy of your rental or lease agreement and receipts of any money paid to a landlord, property management business, or rental company in a safe place.

Have a Backup Plan

Should something go awry, have a plan B in mind. That might include staying at a hotel or motel for several days before you can move into your new home. Perhaps you have a friend or family member in the area—is it possible to stay with them? Have extra cash or a debit card on hand for emergencies and have at least one credit card that can cover unforeseen expenses. You might not have to dip into your contingency finances, but should it be necessary, you definitely want to be prepared.

Insurance

Your landlord may require renter's insurance even though it is not mandated in any state by law. In most cases where the management company or property owner requires rental insurance, you will need to purchase it prior to signing the rental or lease agreement.

There are different types of insurance coverage. Personal property coverage is to your benefit because it may help replace personal belongings, like furniture or clothing, if they're stolen or destroyed. A general misconception is that the landlord is insured so the tenant doesn't need to be. That's false. The landlord's insurance usually covers only the building or unit you live in, not your possessions.

Renter's liability coverage will help cover costs if a visitor is injured or you unintentionally cause damage to someone else's property. Accidents do happen, and this type of policy serves you when they do.

Additional living expense coverage is handy should your apartment become uninhabitable for a covered reason and you have an unanticipated hotel stay. Imagine what would happen to you if the building or unit was damaged by fire or extreme winds. The additional living expense coverage would allow you to relocate while repairs were made.

These types of plans have deductibles and limits for payouts by the insurer. Think about all your belongings and what it would cost to replace them. That will help determine how much coverage you need. Then take some time to review several different policies before deciding which suits you best.

Chapter 2

Services to Have Disconnected

Once you know the logistics of where and when you are going, there are certain items that must be taken care of before the packing ever begins. The goal is to organize chaos into functionality that flows and lessens anxiety and stress.

Pay Attention to the Details before the Move

Specific services need to be disconnected at the old location and connected at the new location. Mail has to be forwarded, and family, friends, and business associates need to know you're moving.

When you're disconnecting services, always ask if you have a refund coming from your initial connection. People forget that several years ago they may have placed a deposit for a service and, in the pandemonium of a move, don't think to inquire if they might have it returned. If the company says no, at least you asked and have an answer. But you might be surprised and discover you have some cash coming back to you.

Disconnecting services is a good time to ask for a letter of reference from the company. You might be able to use it in the future in lieu of a deposit if one is required.

Different locations may have different requirements for connection to a service. Always ask what is necessary for new connections before you schedule them. This will prevent any type of surprise at the time service is acquired.

The following is a list where you can organize, track, and compile pertinent information about the companies that offer services that you will need to disconnect from.

DEVRA'S TIP Schedule services to be disconnected so that they come as close as possible to your departure date. In most cases, services like power and water can be disconnected the day after you leave, ensuring that you'll have continuous access to them as you prepare to move.

If you are leaving a rental property, services may need to be transferred back to the property owner's name. If such a transfer of service is needed, coordinate it with your property manager or landlord to ensure you're not responsible for additional and unnecessary fees.

DEVRA'S TIP Be certain to provide all companies with a forwarding address to prevent delays in paying final bills. Missing that last bill will count against your credit score.

Gas

Company name:_____

Address:_____

_____

Website:_____

Phone:_____

Last payment date:_____Last payment: $_____

Disconnect date:_____ Refund: YES / NO

Account number:_____

Notes:_____

_____

_____

_____

Water

Company name:_____

Address:_____

_____

Website:_____

Phone:_____

Last payment date:_____Last payment: $_____

Disconnect date:_____ Refund: YES / NO

Account number:_____

Notes:_____

_____

_____

_____

Electric

Company name:_____

Address:_____

_____

Website:_____

Phone:_____

Last payment date:_____Last payment: $_____

Disconnect date:_____ Refund: YES / NO

Account number:_____

Notes:_____

_____

_____

_____

Sewer

Company name:_____

Address:_____

_____

Website:_____

Phone:_____

Last payment date:_____Last payment: $_____

Disconnect date:_____ Refund: YES / NO

Account number:_____

Notes:_____

_____

_____

_____

Phone Company (Landline)

Company name:_____

Address:_____

_____

Website:_____

Phone:_____

Last payment date:_____Last payment: $_____

Disconnect date:_____ Refund: YES / NO

Account number:_____

Notes:_____

_____

_____

_____

Cable/Satellite TV

Company name:_____

Address:_____

_____

Website:_____

Phone:_____

Last payment date:_____Last payment: $_____

Disconnect date:_____ Refund: YES / NO

Account number:_____

Notes:_____

_____

_____

_____

Internet

Company name:_____

Address:_____

_____

Website:_____

Phone:_____

Last payment date:_____Last payment: $_____

Disconnect date:_____ Refund: YES / NO

Account number:_____

Notes:_____

_____

_____

_____

Trash and Recycling Pickup

Company name:_____

Address:_____

_____

Website:_____

Phone:_____

Last payment date:_____Last payment: $_____

Last pickup date:_____ Refund: YES / NO

Account number:_____

Notes:_____

_____

_____

_____

Yard Services

Company name:_____

Address:_____

_____

Website:_____

Phone:_____

Last payment date:_____Last payment: $_____

Last date:_____ Refund: YES / NO

Account number:_____

Notes:_____

_____

_____

_____

Newspaper

Company name:_____

Address:_____

_____

Website:_____

Phone:_____

Last payment date:_____Last payment: $_____

Last date:_____ Refund: YES / NO

Account number:_____

Notes:_____

_____

_____

_____

Pest Control

Company name:_____

Address:_____

_____

Website:_____

Phone:_____

Last payment date:_____Last payment: $_____

Last date:_____ Refund: YES / NO

Account number:_____

Notes:_____

_____

_____

_____

Homeowners Association (HOA)

Company name:_____

Address:_____

_____

Website:_____

Phone:_____

Last payment date:_____Last payment: $_____

Last date:_____ Refund: YES / NO

Account number:_____

Notes:_____

_____

_____

_____

Spa/Pool Services

Company name:_____

Address:_____

_____

Website:_____

Phone:_____

Last payment date:_____Last payment: $_____

Last date:_____ Refund: YES / NO

Account number:_____

Notes:_____

_____

_____

_____

Cleaning Company/Individual

Company name:_____

Address:_____

_____

Website:_____

Phone:_____

Last payment date:_____Last payment: $_____

Last date:_____ Refund: YES / NO

Account number:_____

Notes:_____

_____

_____

_____

Additional Services to Disconnect

Company name:_____

Address:_____

_____

Website:_____

Phone:_____

Last payment date:_____Last payment: $_____

Last date:_____ Refund: YES / NO

Account number:_____

Notes:_____

_____

_____

_____

Additional Services to Disconnect

Company name:_____

Address:_____

_____

Website:_____

Phone:_____

Last payment date:_____Last payment: $_____

End date:_____ Refund: YES / NO

Account number:_____

Notes:_____

_____

_____

_____

_____

Company name:_____

Address:_____

_____

Website:_____

Phone:_____

Last payment date:_____Last payment: $_____

End date:_____ Refund: YES / NO

Account number:_____

Notes:_____

_____

_____

_____

_____

Rental or Homeowner's Insurance

If you are planning a self-move, it is important to find out if your belongings will be insured during transit. Be sure to verify this through your insurance company.

Company name:_____

Address:_____

_____

Website:_____

Phone:_____

Last payment date:_____Last payment: $_____

End of coverage date:_____ Refund: YES / NO

Account number:_____

Notes:_____

_____

_____

Safety Deposit Box and Storage Units

DEVRA'S TIP As odd as it may seem, people forget they have safety deposit boxes or a spot in a storage facility. If you have a safety deposit box, be sure to secure the contents and close it out, and don't forget belongings in an off-site storage unit.

Safety Deposit

Bank Location:_____

_____

Date closed:_____

Storage Unit

Location:_____

_____

Date closed:_____

Once you know where you will be living, check to see if there is a local chamber of commerce. If there is, request a new resident package. These usually include directories, restaurant guides, a map of the area, and information related to living in the new area. They are very helpful when settling in a new city, especially when preparing to have specific services connected. You might even be able to request the package online, saving you a trip when you arrive in your new city or town.

Chapter 3

Services to Schedule for Connection

Now that you know when you are leaving and where you are going and have notified services to be disconnected on a specific date, think about your future needs and what services will need to be arranged prior to your arrival.

Appointments to connect to services may vary from requiring three days' notice to needing several weeks, depending on the location. Plan ahead! You don't want to arrive at your new home and have no power or water. Some companies will require a person to be present when services are connected or activated—be sure to ask whether someone must be present.

If either natural gas or propane was completely disconnected from the new property, it may be necessary for a gas company employee to do a thorough inspection and light pilots on all older gas-powered appliances. This may not be true for all gas appliances, but it's always a good idea to make sure they are in top-notch working order. An adult will need to be present for this process.

Electricity and water can usually be connected and turned on without an adult being present to sign off on any documents. Always verify before the appointment whether the utility company requires a signature from someone over the age of eighteen at the time of connection.

Cable and satellite companies require an adult to be present for their installation and testing. If you're handy and adventurous, you can order a self-installation satellite kit. However, if wiring or positioning the dish sounds challenging, it may be best to have a professional complete the installation.

Wi-Fi is something that you can usually set up yourself once you have a provider. Most modems come with step-by-step instructions.

Once Wi-Fi is enabled, the company representative may need to test signal strength on your devices. You will need to have them set up and ready to receive.

DEVRA'S TIP If you are concerned about a Wi-Fi connection, speak with your cellular provider about a personal hot spot. Find out if you have one. If you don't, you might consider temporarily adding it to your plan. A personal hot spot works by tapping into a cellular network and then wirelessly sharing a data connection with other nearby Wi-Fi–enabled devices. They may not run at the speed you're accustomed to, but the hot spot will give you a fairly reliable connection to the internet. Depending on your cellular company and the plan you have, you may have to pay for the data used, as well as regular data use.

Gas

Company name:_____

Address:_____

_____

Website:_____

_____

Phone:_____

Contact Person:_____

Date to be connected:_____

Notes:_____

_____

_____

_____

Water

Company name:_____

Address:_____

_____

Website:_____

_____

Phone:_____

Contact Person:_____

Date to be connected:_____

Notes:_____

_____

_____

_____

Electric

Company name:_____

Address:_____

_____

Website:_____

_____

Phone:_____

Contact Person:_____

Date to be connected:_____

Notes:_____

_____

_____

_____

Sewer

Company name:_____

Address:_____

_____

Website:_____

_____

Phone:_____

Contact Person:_____

Date to be connected:_____

Notes:_____

_____

_____

_____

Phone Company (Landline)

Company name:_____

Address:_____

_____

Website:_____

_____

Phone:_____

Contact Person:_____

Date to be connected:_____

Notes:_____

_____

_____

_____

Rental or Homeowner's Insurance

Company name:_____

Address:_____

_____

Website:_____

_____

Phone:_____

Contact Person:_____

Date to be effective:_____

Notes:_____

_____

_____

_____

Cable/Satellite TV

Company name:_____

Address:_____

_____

Website:_____

_____

Phone:_____

Contact Person:_____

Date to be connected:_____

Notes:_____

_____

_____

_____

Internet

Company name:_____

Address:_____

_____

Website:_____

_____

Phone:_____

Contact Person:_____

Date to be connected:_____

Notes:_____

_____

_____

_____

Trash and Recycling Pickup

Company name:_____

Address:_____

_____

Website:_____

_____

Phone:_____

Contact Person:_____

Start date:_____

Notes:_____

_____

_____

_____

Yard Services

Company name:_____

Address:_____

_____

Website:_____

_____

Phone:_____

Contact Person:_____

Start Date:_____

Notes:_____

_____

_____

_____

Newspaper

Company name:_____

Address:_____

_____

Website:_____

_____

Phone:_____

Contact Person:_____

Start date:_____

Notes:_____

_____

_____

_____

Pest Control

Company name:_____

Address:_____

_____

Website:_____

_____

Phone:_____

Contact Person:_____

Start date:_____

Notes:_____

_____

_____

_____

Homeowners Association (HOA)

Company name:_____

Address:_____

_____

Website:_____

_____

Phone:_____

Contact Person:_____

Start date:_____

Notes:_____

_____

_____

_____

Spa/Pool Services

Company name:_____

Address:_____

_____

Website:_____

_____

Phone:_____

Contact Person:_____

Start date:_____

Notes:_____

_____

_____

_____

Cleaning Company/Individual

Company name:_____

Address:_____

_____

Website:_____

_____

Phone:_____

Contact Person:_____

Start date:_____

Notes:_____

_____

_____

_____

Additional Services to Connect

Company name:_____

Address:_____

_____

Website:_____

_____

Phone:_____

Contact Person:_____

Date to be connected:_____

Notes:_____

_____

_____

_____

_____

Company name:_____

Address:_____

_____

Website:_____

_____

Phone:_____

Contact Person:_____

Date to be connected:_____

Notes:_____

_____

_____

_____

_____

Additional Services to Connect

Company name:_____

Address:_____

_____

Website:_____

_____

Phone:_____

Contact Person:_____

Date to be connected:_____

Notes:_____

_____

_____

_____

_____

Chapter 4

Who to Notify of Your Move

As you share the good news of your move with family, friends, and business associates, jot down their names so you don't leave anyone out.

Family

_____

_____

_____

_____

_____

Friends

_____

_____

_____

_____

_____

Business Associates

_____

_____

_____

_____

_____

Cell Phone Company

Company name:_____

Address:_____

_____

Website:_____

_____

Phone:_____

Contact person: _____

Date notified:_____

Notes:_____

_____

_____

_____

Who Else to Notify of Your Change of Address

The United States Post Office (USPS)

A change-of-address form is required so that items such as bills, bank statements, and other mail can be forwarded to your new address.

There is a small identity validation fee for a change of address through the online system of the United States Post Office. A major credit card is required for this process. However, if you go into the post office and make the change, there is no fee. If you're moving out of the country, it is necessary to make the forwarding application in person at your post office.

It's recommended that you request mail be sent to the new address beginning the day before your scheduled arrival. This will prevent an interruption of mail services. First-Class Mail® and Priority Mail® service will forward mail to your new address for a period of twelve months. Periodicals, such as magazines and newsletters, are only forwarded for sixty days, which provides ample time for you to notify the publishers of any subscriptions you have.

List the full name of all family members in your household on the forwarding request. You will need one change-of-address (COA) form if all members of the family have the same last name. If members of the family have different last names, you need a COA form for each member of the family with a different last name. If you received business mail at your old address, you will need a COA form for the business too. Be sure to check the box that lists your new address as permanent.

Date of forward request:_____

Date forwarding begins:_____

Notes:_____

_____

_____

_____

Bank or Credit Union

If you are traveling across state lines and will be using credit cards or ATMs, let your bank know what states you will be in. Although some financial institutions will contact you via phone, text, or email when they notice charges from unusual locations, some simply deactivate your card instead. The simple step of calling or going online to note that you will be traveling will ensure the bank doesn't freeze your account to prevent fraud.

Bank name:_____

Website: _____

Phone:_____

Type of account(s):_____

Date of address change:_____

Notes:_____

_____

_____

Bank name:_____

Website: _____

Phone:_____

Type of account(s):_____

Date of address change:_____

Notes:_____

_____

_____

_____

Bank name:_____

Website: _____

Phone:_____

Type of account(s):_____

Date of address change:_____

Notes:_____

_____

_____

_____

Credit Cards

Notify credit card companies that you will be traveling so that they will not freeze your accounts for possible fraud. If you are traveling across state lines, let the card companies know which states.

Company name: _____

Website: _____

Phone:_____

Contact:_____

Date of address change:_____

Notes:_____

_____

Company name: _____

Website: _____

Phone:_____

Contact:_____

Date of address change:_____

Notes:_____

_____

Company name: _____

Website: _____

Phone:_____

Contact:_____

Date of address change:_____

Notes:_____

_____

Company name: _____

Website: _____

Phone:_____

Contact:_____

Date of address change:_____

Phone:_____

Notes:_____

_____

Company name: _____

Website: _____

Phone:_____

Contact:_____

Date of address change:_____

Notes:_____

_____

Company name: _____

Website: _____

Phone:_____

Contact:_____

Date of address change:_____

Notes:_____

_____

_____

_____

Subscriptions

Company name: _____

Website: _____

Phone:_____

Contact:_____

Date of address change:_____

Notes:_____

_____

_____

_____

Company name: _____

Website: _____

Phone:_____

Contact:_____

Date of address change:_____

Notes:_____

_____

_____

_____

Subscriptions

Company name: _____

Website: _____

Phone:_____

Contact:_____

Date of address change:_____

Notes:_____

_____

_____

_____

Company name: _____

Website: _____

Phone:_____

Contact:_____

Date of address change:_____

Notes:_____

_____

_____

_____

_____

Company name: _____

Website: _____

Phone:_____

Contact:_____

Date of address change:_____

Notes:_____

_____

_____

_____

_____

Warranties

These should include electronic devices, appliances, and other items you might have secured warranties for at the time of purchase.

Company name: _____

Website: _____

Phone:_____

Contact:_____

Date of address change:_____

Notes:_____

_____

_____

_____

Company name: _____

Website: _____

Phone:_____

Contact:_____

Date of address change:_____

Notes:_____

_____

_____

_____

Company name: _____

Website: _____

Phone:_____

Contact:_____

Date of address change:_____

Notes:_____

_____

_____

Warranties

Company name: _____

Website: _____

Phone:_____

Contact:_____

Date of address change:_____

Notes:_____

_____

_____

_____

_____

Company name: _____

Website: _____

Phone:_____

Contact:_____

Date of address change:_____

Notes:_____

_____

_____

_____

_____

Company name: _____

Website: _____

Phone:_____

Contact:_____

Date of address change:_____

Notes:_____

_____

_____

_____

DEVRA'S TIP: Keep your log-in and password information safe by using an online password manager like Password Boss, 1Password, or Dashlane. You can also safely store and access passwords on your smartphone using the iCloud keychain on Apple or Android devices or on your desktop Mac or Windows computer. Using a browser like Chrome also allows you to use their keychain password manager, which is always secure. Another option is to keep information on a flash drive or written out in a separate notebook that you keep locked in a fireproof safe. It's a good investment to have a small safe (small means movable) available at home for important papers, like Social Security cards, birth and marriage records, and so on.

Chapter 5

Collect and Compile Important Papers

Before you begin packing, collect your important paperwork and make a plan to keep it easily accessible during your transit from location to location. First, scan or photograph all your documents and store them on a digital device as a backup. All records such as driver's licenses, vehicle registrations, Social Security cards, checkbooks, divorce and child custody documents, passports, and insurance cards should be carried with you. Some documents such as marriage licenses and birth certificates don't have to be carried on your person. Instead, put them in a watertight container that travels with you, not in a moving van or rental truck.

These items should be with you and easy to access during your move. Check them off the list as you collect them.

___ Driver's license	___ Auto insurance card
___ Social Security card	___ Passport
___ TSA/GOES card	___ Medical insurance card
___ Secondary medical card	___ Child custody papers
___ Divorce papers	___ Checkbooks
___ Credit cards	___ Personal phonebook
___ Spare glasses	___ Supplements
___ Prescription medications	___ Unfilled prescriptions*

Always carry current medications with you while in transit.

DEVRA'S TIP: As a just-in-case, people who are moving often request that their physicians write new prescriptions that can be filled one time after the move is completed and they are in their new location. Some prescriptions cannot be transferred between pharmacies, which is why it is wise to have the paper prescription from the doctor.

Some naturopathic doctors' prescriptions may not be honored or filled in some states. If you see a naturopathic physician, be sure to have your medicines filled before leaving. Have enough on hand to hold you over until you can find a new naturopath. The prescription list on page 75 should include your naturopathic prescriptions.

Family Medical

No one anticipates the need for one's medical history during a move, but it's good to have it available. The following pages are a place to note important health information. Keep this book with you while in transit, and should an emergency arise, you will have details of your and your family's past medical care handy.

Once you've relocated, you'll need to find a new physician, and that person will want as much information about you and your family as possible. Will you remember the name of the doctor or clinic that performed your last blood work, colonoscopy, or mammogram? Or the orthopedic surgeon and facility that x-rayed and treated your child's broken leg when they slid into first base five years ago? Unless you've repeatedly used the same doctor and clinic for a number of years, you probably don't have that information embedded in your mind. It's one of those things most people don't keep track of over time; we never give a thought to it until we're asked about it. However, when you move, it is beneficial to have those older records in hand.

New doctors, even general practitioners, will want a full medical history on you and the members of your family. Having the name, address, and phone numbers handy for your past doctors, hospital ER visits, and imaging centers will make it easier on your new physicians. When you provide doctors with thorough data, they can better treat you as a patient.

Be aware that you can always request a copy of your records at the time of treatment, including copies of medical images, like x-rays. Generally, people don't make that request, and over time, details can get hazy. At the very least, you should know the name of the facility that took the images and where they are located.

Before you move, ask your physicians to provide you with a means of transferring your medical records. They may prefer to copy records onto a USB drive or CD, or they may have another means of transferring them to you or your new doctor. These records should include any x-rays, MRIs, DEXA scans (bone density tests), CT scans, and all other records and images. Digital devices are much easier to transport and secure. Should your physician be old-school and provide hard copies, pack them in a waterproof plastic container that can travel in your personal luggage. Don't pack them in a box that can be damaged or misplaced during a move.

If you cannot physically access your records, be sure to sign a medical release form with all your physicians before you move. This is best done in the physician's office. This way, when the time comes, your previous doctor will have the documents ready for the new doctor to access. If you wait until after the move to request a medical release form, you may have to wait for the form to make it to you or the new doctor. In some cases, time is imperative, which makes assembling this information vital before the move.

On the following pages you can list current physicians, specialists, dentists, and so on. This will help you and your new doctors once you've settled in your new home.

Your General Physician

Name of patient: _____

Allergies: _____

Name of doctor: _____

Name of clinic: _____

Website: _____

Address: _____

Phone: _____ FAX/email: _____

Date last seen: _____

Notes: _____

_____

_____

_____

_____

General Physician for Your Spouse/Partner

Name of patient: _____

Allergies: _____

Name of doctor: _____

Name of clinic: _____

Website: _____

Address: _____

Phone: _____ FAX/email: _____

Date last seen: _____

Notes: _____

_____

_____

_____

_____

Pediatrician

Name of patient: _____

Allergies: _____

Name of doctor: _____

Name of clinic: _____

Website: _____

Address: _____

Phone: _____ FAX/email: _____

Date last seen: _____

Notes: _____

_____

_____

_____

_____

_____

Name of patient: _____

Allergies: _____

Name of doctor: _____

Name of clinic: _____

Website: _____

Address: _____

Phone: _____ FAX/email: _____

Date last seen: _____

Notes: _____

_____

_____

_____

_____

_____

Name of patient: _____

Allergies: _____

Name of doctor: _____

Name of clinic: _____

Website: _____

Address: _____

Phone: _____ FAX/email: _____

Date last seen: _____

Notes: _____

_____

_____

_____

Children's Records

Child's name: _____

Allergies: _____

Vaccination record: _____

_____

_____

Illnesses: _____

_____

_____

Injuries: _____

_____

_____

Notes: _____

_____

_____

_____

Children's Records

Child's name: _____

Allergies: _____

Vaccination record: _____

_____

_____

Illnesses: _____

_____

_____

Injuries: _____

_____

_____

Notes: _____

_____

_____

_____

Child's name: _____

Allergies: _____

Vaccination record: _____

_____

_____

Illnesses: _____

_____

_____

Injuries: _____

_____

_____

Notes: _____

_____

_____

_____

Child's name: _____

Allergies: _____

Vaccination record: _____

_____

_____

Illnesses: _____

_____

_____

Injuries: _____

_____

_____

Notes: _____

_____

_____

_____

Naturopath

Name of patient(s): _____

Allergies: _____

Name of doctor: _____

Name of clinic: _____

Address: _____

Phone: _____ FAX/email: _____

Last date seen: _____

Notes: _____

_____

_____

_____

_____

_____

_____

Specialists

(Such as oncologist, dermatologist, orthopedic specialist, OB-GYN, internist, etc.)

Name of patient: _____

Name of doctor: _____

Specialty: _____

Name of clinic: _____

Website: _____

Address: _____

Phone: _____ FAX/email: _____

Date last seen: _____

Notes: _____

_____

_____

_____

_____

Name of patient: _____

Name of doctor: _____

Specialty: _____

Name of clinic: _____

Website: _____

Address: _____

Phone: _____ FAX/email: _____

Date last seen: _____

Notes: _____

_____

_____

_____

_____

Name of patient: _____

Name of doctor: _____

Specialty: _____

Name of clinic: _____

Website: _____

Address: _____

Phone: _____ FAX/email: _____

Date last seen: _____

Notes: _____

_____

_____

_____

_____

_____

_____

Chiropractor

Name of patient: _____

Name of doctor: _____

Name of clinic: _____

Website: _____

Address: _____

Phone: _____ FAX/email: _____

Date last seen: _____

Notes: _____

_____

_____

_____

_____

_____

Your Dentist

Name of patient: _____

Name of dentist: _____

Name of clinic: _____

Website: _____

Address: _____

Phone: _____ FAX/email: _____

Date last seen: _____

Notes: _____

_____

_____

_____

_____

_____

Dentist for Your Spouse/Partner

Name of patient: _____

Name of dentist: _____

Name of clinic: _____

Website: _____

Address: _____

Phone: _____ FAX/email: _____

Date last seen: _____

Notes: _____

_____

_____

_____

_____

_____

Children's Dentist

Name of patient: _____

Name of dentist: _____

Name of clinic: _____

Website: _____

Address: _____

Phone: _____ FAX/email: _____

Date last seen: _____

Notes: _____

_____

_____

_____

_____

_____

_____

Name of patient: _____

Name of dentist: _____

Name of clinic: _____

Website: _____

Address: _____

Phone: _____ FAX/email: _____

Date last seen: _____

Notes: _____

_____

_____

_____

_____

_____

_____

Orthodontist

Name of patient: _____

Name of orthodontist: _____

Name of clinic: _____

Website: _____

Address: _____

Phone: _____ FAX/email: _____

Date last seen: _____

Notes: _____

_____

_____

_____

_____

_____

_____

Oral Surgeon

Name of patient: _____

Name of doctor: _____

Name of clinic: _____

Website: _____

Address: _____

Phone: _____ FAX/email: _____

Date last seen: _____

Notes: _____

_____

_____

_____

_____

_____

_____

Ophthalmologist/Optometrist

Name of patient(s): _____

Name of doctor: _____

Name of clinic: _____

Website: _____

Address: _____

Phone: _____ FAX/email: _____

Date last seen: _____

Notes: _____

_____

Hospital/ER Visits

Name of patient: _____

Name of hospital: _____

Website: _____

Address: _____

Phone: _____ FAX/email: _____

Date of visit: _____

Reason for visit: _____

Notes: _____

_____

Name of patient: _____

Name of hospital: _____

Website: _____

Address: _____

Phone: _____ FAX/email: _____

Date of visit: _____

Reason for visit: _____

Notes: _____

_____

Hospital/ER Visits

Name of patient: _____

Name of hospital: _____

Website: _____

Address: _____

Phone: _____ FAX/email: _____

Date of visit: _____

Reason for visit: _____

Notes: _____

_____

_____

Name of patient: _____

Name of hospital: _____

Website: _____

Address: _____

Phone: _____ FAX/email: _____

Date of visit: _____

Reason for visit: _____

Notes: _____

_____

_____

Medical Imagery

Ask your doctors to transfer these images to you in whatever method their offices prefer. That may be a digital copy of this information, a copy on CD, or a USB drive for your new doctor, or they may prefer to send it digitally.

Name of patient: _____

Ordered by: _____

Location of service: _____

Website: _____

Address: _____

Phone: _____ FAX/email: _____

Date of services: _____

Type of image: _____

Notes: _____

_____

Name of patient: _____

Ordered by: _____

Location of service: _____

Website: _____

Address: _____

Phone: _____ FAX/email: _____

Date of services: _____

Type of image: _____

Notes: _____

_____

Name of patient: _____

Ordered by: _____

Location of service: _____

Website: _____

Address: _____

Phone: _____ FAX/email: _____

Date of services: _____

Type of image: _____

Notes: _____

_____

Name of patient: _____

Ordered by: _____

Location of service: _____

Website: _____

Address: _____

Phone: _____ FAX/email: _____

Date of services: _____

Type of image: _____

Notes: _____

_____

_____

Name of patient: _____

Ordered by: _____

Location of service: _____

Website: _____

Address: _____

Phone: _____ FAX/email: _____

Date of services: _____

Type of image: _____

Notes: _____

_____

_____

Pharmacy

Name of pharmacist: _____

Pharmacy address: _____

Website: _____

Address: _____

Phone: _____ FAX/email: _____

Notes: _____

_____

Prescriptions

When moving out of state, know the laws. For example, medicinal marijuana is legal in some states but not in all. A prescription for medicinal marijuana may be valid in the state you're leaving but not the one you're moving to, and it is illegal to carry marijuana, medicinal or not, across state lines.

List all current prescriptions, including patient, prescription number, and pharmacy.

Medication	Patient	Prescription Number	Pharmacy

Medication	Patient	Prescription Number	Pharmacy

Pets' Medical

Pets are part of the family, and their medical history is important too. Make certain their vaccinations are up-to-date before you move. If you are moving out of state, be sure that the pet is welcome and find out if a quarantine period is required. An example is Hawaii, which has strict rabies laws for dogs and cats. Hamsters, gerbils, ferrets, bearded dragons, and monkeys are among the types of pets that are not welcome in all states. Laws do change, so always verify what restrictions might apply in your new state.

Your current vet should be able to provide a copy of your pets' medical history in either digital format or hard copy. It's also a good idea to have a photograph and description of your pets with you in case they wander off and get lost.

Name of pet: _____ Breed: _____

Microchip number: _____

Microchip company name: _____

Name of clinic: _____ Vet: _____

Website: _____

Address: _____

Phone: _____ FAX/email: _____

Vaccination record: _____

_____

Illness: _____

Injuries: _____

Medication(s): _____

Home Again contact number: _____

Notes: _____

_____

_____

_____

Pets' Medical

Name of pet: _____ Breed: _____

Microchip number: _____

Microchip company name: _____

Name of clinic: _____ Vet: _____

Website: _____

Address: _____

Phone: _____ FAX/email: _____

Vaccination record: _____

_____

Illness: _____

Injuries: _____

Medication(s): _____

Home Again contact number: _____

Notes: _____

_____

Name of pet: _____ Breed: _____

Microchip number: _____

Microchip company name: _____

Name of clinic: _____ Vet: _____

Website: _____

Address: _____

Phone: _____ FAX/email: _____

Vaccination record: _____

_____

Illness: _____

Injuries: _____

Medication(s): _____

Home Again contact number: _____

Notes: _____

_____

Name of pet: _____ Breed: _____

Microchip number: _____

Microchip company name: _____

Name of clinic: _____ Vet: _____

Website: _____

Address: _____

Phone: _____ FAX/email: _____

Vaccination record: _____

_____

Illness: _____

Injuries: _____

Medication(s): _____

Home Again contact number: _____

Notes: _____

_____

_____

_____

_____

DEVRA'S TIP When you, your spouse/partner, child, or pet visit a new physician, take this book with you. All your medical information will be here for them.

Additional Documents

These documents can be packed in clearly marked, waterproof containers, but it's wise to have digital copies of them on a USB drive that you can carry with you or put in your luggage. They can also be stored on your computer or securely saved online.

___ Birth certificates

___ Marriage license

___ Death certificates

___ Family history

___ Bank statements

___ Paystubs

___Insurance policies (company names): _____

_____

___ Legal documents

___ Settlement paperwork

___ Tax records for last seven years

___ Education history for adults (schools): _____

_____

___ Grade transcripts for children: (grade and school): _____

_____

___ Diplomas

___ Employment history

___ Additional vehicle registrations: _____

_____

___ Credit card statements

PART 2

PREPARING TO MOVE

Chapter 6

Determining the Best Way to Move

How Much Stuff Do You Have?

Humans tend to be collectors. Don't let that inclination make your move more difficult or costly than it needs to be. Determine what is moving with you. Are there things you've considered selling or giving as a donation? If your new home has a washer, dryer, and refrigerator, you may not want to haul the old ones across the state. If it doesn't, in some cases, it might be a good idea to sell items such as washers and dryers and purchase new ones once you're settled. Maybe you haven't gotten around to cleaning out the closets lately and there are things hiding in corners that can go to a donation center to be helpful to someone else. Old towels and blankets that you don't use to protect furniture during the move are always welcome at animal shelters. Maybe you've wanted to hold a garage sale? Now might be the time to do just that. Or list items for sale on resale apps and social media.

Give your residence a walk-through and decide what you must take with you. Then downsize.

When Should You Move?

Because of school-age children, most people try to move during the summer months, between Memorial Day and Labor Day. That span of time is going to be the busiest for truck rentals and moving lines, which makes time management even more important.

You can estimate that one in every five people will move each year, and most of them will move during the summer. In fact, according to MovingLabor.com, 80 percent of moves within the US each year occur between April and September.[2] Then take into consideration that most leases are up at the end of the month and the fact that people who are moving usually try to accommodate their work hours by moving on a weekend. That means that it might be difficult to arrange for a truck rental or professional moving company on weekends during the summer. Seasonal pricing is common and prices are more expensive "in season," which are summer months.

If you must do a summer move, the solution might be to arrange for the truck rental or moving company well in advance and schedule the move during off days, Sunday through Thursday.

How Do You Get There?

The next big decision is who will move your belongings. Will it be a self-move or handled through a moving company? Most people prefer a self-move, primarily because most people are on a budget.

Look around your home or apartment. How many material possessions have you accumulated? How much are you taking with you? Is it a quick move from one part of the city to another? Or is it cross-country? Are you cost-conscious? These are all questions that help determine which type of move suits you best.

Determining the means by which you want to make the transition depends greatly on the size of your residence. Moving a two-bedroom, two-bath apartment that you've been in for a year or two is much different than moving a four-bedroom, three-bath house that has been your home for thirty years. A two-bedroom apartment can be moved in a rental truck or trailer, but the furniture and possessions that occupy a big house will probably require several containers or a professional moving company.

Chapter 7
Moving Yourself

We had the opportunity to pose some questions to Jeff Lockridge, Manager of Media and Public Relations for U-Haul®, a widely recognized self-move organization. When we asked, "What are the primary reasons people prefer self-moving?" he responded with the following:

A self-move almost always offers substantial cost savings over a full-service move. Full-service moves require that you pay for labor services, including drivers for the moving equipment, loading and unloading, packing and unpacking, etc. A do-it-yourself (DIY) move means you are paying for a rental truck or trailer, gas if you rent a truck, and likely a very small fee for damage coverage on the rental equipment. Mileage is included in the price of one-way U-Haul® trucks and trailers. If you are planning an in-town move, a DIY move is a no-brainer. If you are moving cross-country, your cost savings by choosing a DIY move could be thousands of dollars.

Aside from our customers keeping more of their money, we find that DIY movers gain peace of mind by having direct control over, and constant access to, their belongings. Many U-Haul® customers like the convenience and certainty that comes with having their valued personal possessions in the truck they are driving or the trailer they are towing.

Another appealing factor of the self-move is the contactless option. U-Haul Truck Share 24/7® was introduced to allow our customers to reserve a truck, pick up the truck, and return the truck entirely on a smart phone or internet-connected device with GPS and camera features. This time-saving program allows customers to rent any time of the day while avoiding lines at the counter. Customers communicate directly with U-Haul Live Verify[SM] agents at the company's headquarters in Phoenix. Once a customer arrives at the pickup location, an agent confirms the customer's identity and location, provides a numbered code for the key box, and the customer is on their way after verifying the truck's condition and fuel levels. U-Haul Truck Share 24/7®, which was implemented years before the pandemic, gained newfound popularity and traction when contactless options became the norm for many businesses in 2020.

The average person moves at least eleven times in a lifetime. Many of those moves will be self-moves. Thus, almost everyone has a U-Haul® story. U-Haul® customers are often repeat customers, and they know our number one priority is the safety of every individual and family using our equipment, as well as the safety of their belongings, on their journey to their next destination in life.[3]

Recognized by *Newsweek* as America's number one company for customer service in the Moving Services industry for 2020,[4] U-Haul® is probably the most recognized name in the self-moving industry. Over several decades, they have implemented numerous different ways to assist their customers.

In 2008, U-Haul® CEO Joe Shoen gave out his cell phone number on a national TV news program, letting customers know they could call him personally if they had an issue. Mr. Shoen still takes calls and responds to customers' emails when possible.

U-Haul® understands customer service is the backbone of any successful business. While we were founded because

L. S. "Sam" and Anna Mary Carty Shoen identified a need in the marketplace that was not being met—the need for accessible, affordable residential mobility—we would not be an industry leader nearly 80 years later without caring for our customers and providing quality service. U-Haul® exists because of its DIY moving and self-storage customers, and we must continue to listen to our customers and let them tell us what products and services they need—and how we can best provide those.

U-Haul® Team Members and local dealers are often the first people new residents meet or speak to when they arrive in a different city with our rental equipment. Our people relish that role and strive to make the best impression possible . . . not just for our business but for our communities.

Prospective customers can always visit uhaul.com to read verified customer reviews of any U-Haul® rental location. Our reviews—the good and the bad—are 100 percent authentic and completely unedited. You won't find a fake review facilitated by a third-party site to enhance online visibility and traffic. We take the honest route.[5]

Consider...

There are several things to consider with a self-move. Cost is one of them. Following is a general outline of costs to anticipate and a budget estimate for your move.

Rental Trucks

The rental truck will probably be the biggest expense. Rental trucks come in various sizes, and the fee is based on the size of the vehicle and your start and end points. Call the major companies and ask about truck sizes, fees, and discounts. Sometimes companies offer military and student discounts. Organizations such as AAA, AARP, and employee associations may also provide membership discounts.

> **DEVRA'S TIP** If you are going to be doing a self-move with a rental truck, clear an area or room in your home and tape off the dimensions of the truck on the floor. This can be done easily with masking tape. As you pack boxes, place them in the boundary taped on the floor. As you fill the area, keep in mind the height of the truck or container.
>
> This way you will see what is going to fit in the space when you start loading the truck the day of the move. It also gives you an opportunity to move things around so that nothing will be left behind.

The sizes of rental trucks range from a cargo van to a 26-foot truck. Each size has a weight and capacity limit. A cargo van has a weight limit of 3,500 pounds and a capacity limit of 404 cubic feet. A 22-foot truck has a weight limit of 10,000 pounds and a capacity of 1,200 cubic feet. After you estimate the cubic feet to be moved, speak with the rental agency to determine what size is best for you.

Courtesy of U-Haul®

Some trucks have ramps; some don't. A ramp makes it much easier to load, whether it's by carrying boxes by hand or on a dolly.

Rental Trailers

Cargo or utility trailers might be an option if you haven't accumulated a lot of belongings. Like trucks, cargo trailers and utility trailers come in a variety of sizes and can serve anything from an across-town move to a cross-country self-move. The upside to a rental trailer is that it may save you some money over a truck rental. However, you have to have a vehicle with a trailer hitch and the power to pull.

Insurance

Be smart. Don't try to save money by avoiding additional insurance. Should you have an accident during your move, having insurance will be worthwhile. Check with your personal insurance agent to determine what additional coverage you might need. Ask for a quote from the truck rental company you select.

Fuel

You will be responsible for the purchase of gas during your move, and you'll also be expected to return the truck with a full tank. If you're moving between states, this cost can be difficult to estimate, as gas prices can vary greatly between states and even towns. Websites and apps such as Gas Buddy may help save a few cents per gallon on your fuel costs by providing the lowest prices in the area you are traveling through. Always estimate high to be on the safe side.

Fuel tank capacity varies with the size of the truck, and miles per gallon (mpg) on a rental truck is low. Fully loaded, you can expect about twelves miles per gallon.

Lodging and Food

If you're moving to a location more than one day away, you will need to plan on meals and lodging for the journey. Add in at least two extra days of expenses, as you might encounter unexpected delays, such as a vehicle breakdown, bad weather, or illness.

If you can map your route and estimate the drive time, you might be able to save a little money by making reservations along the route. If you are traveling with pets, be sure to know which motels or hotels will accept animals. This can save you a lot of time driving around searching for lodging for the night.

Towing Rentals

You can tow your car behind the rental truck. There are additional charges for a car trailer and a tow dolly, as well as other towing and moving accessories. It's best to speak with the rental agency about extra items you may need and their price. Also plan on additional fuel costs.

Loading and Unloading

You may need help loading and/or unloading the rental truck. U-Haul® has an affiliation with Moving Help®. U-Haul® told us, "Moving Help® is an online marketplace powered by U-Haul® where customers can find, review, price and hire thousands of independent local Moving Help Service Providers® for the time, date, location and number of labor providers needed."[6]

Other companies have independent contracts with individuals who provide this service. If it is available, the cost will vary and depend on the location and availability.

If you want to do it all yourself and don't have access to a utility dolly, rent one. It's worth every penny not to have to cart and carry heavy boxes.

Will Everything Fit in a Truck?

How much space will be needed in a truck or container? Some companies suggest that you estimate 400 to 450 cubic feet per average room. If it's a large room or you have a lot of stuff in it, estimate high. Cubic feet measure the volume of space, while square footage measures the area as a flat surface. You'll be dealing with volume because household items come in a variety of sizes and shapes.

Calculate the Size of a Truck

It's generally recommended to measure in cubic feet, as this takes height, length, and width of the truck or container into consideration. To calculate cubic feet, multiply the length by the width by the height. You're estimating how large the rental truck or container will need to be, so add 10 to 15 percent to your assessment to guarantee ample room.

Here are general estimates of truck size that you can use once you estimate the cubic feet space you'll need:

- cargo van (400 cubic feet): 1 room, studio apartment
- 10-to-12-foot truck (450 cubic feet): 1–2 rooms
- 15-to-17-foot truck (800 cubic feet): 2–3 rooms
- 20-to-22-foot truck (1,200 cubic feet): 3–5 rooms
- 26-foot truck (1,700 cubic feet): 5–7 rooms

Thoughts on Rental Trucks

How's your driving? Towing a car behind a rental truck or even driving a large truck can be daunting if you've never done it. Parking can be a nightmare. Always ask for tips and a tutorial from your rental agency. Don't worry about whether the counter person is going to judge you for your lack of skill or experience. It's in their best interest, and yours, to help you navigate the ins and outs of maneuvering an oversized vehicle.

We asked U-Haul® how they help put people's minds at ease when they aren't accustomed to driving a large vehicle. Here is their response:

> While U-Haul® trucks are easier to drive than you may think, they require a cautious and considerate approach. Getting behind the wheel of a smaller box truck will feel a lot like driving a pickup truck. Larger models will seem like a bit more, but the same safety principles apply. Be a defensive driver. Slow down and take your time—don't look to pass other drivers. Adjust and utilize your side mirrors. Give yourself additional time to brake when approaching a stop. Give yourself ample space to turn and switch lanes. Make sure there is extra distance between your truck and the vehicle in front of you. If you are pulling a trailer, load the trailer properly before embarking. (Proper loading means at least 60 percent of your cargo weight in the front of the trailer—toward the tongue— for a secure center of gravity. This will help you avoid sway, aka fishtailing.) These tips can reduce stress behind the wheel and ensure a safe trip.[7]

Courtesy of U-Haul®

Devra was inexperienced at towing a car behind a rental truck. Her story illustrates one of many reasons why it is important to know how to handle a larger vehicle, especially with a car in tow.

As we had lost 90 percent of our possessions in a tornado and hadn't acquired much during our short stay in the state of Washington, we rented a truck and a car tow dolly, loaded our few belongings, and set out for another new beginning.

I rented a truck that had a door between the cab and the storage compartment; that way we could save money and sleep in the back of the truck. With mattresses loaded in the truck last and piled atop the boxes in back, we headed down Highway 101.

The day wore on, and I felt drowsy. I spotted a parking lot where I felt we'd be safe and pulled over to get some sleep. There wasn't much room between our noses and the roof of the truck, but it would do. Or so we thought.

Before dawn, the rhythm of pounding rain reverberated through the truck. To make matters worse, the truck had gotten very cold and was radiating a chill through its interior. Trying to ignore the deafening sound, my daughter rolled over and felt water pooling on the mattress next to her. The roof was leaking!

When we finally gave in to the noise, leaks, and chill and crawled back into the cab, I realized I had parked the vehicle in a way that prevented me from pulling forward. And I had no idea how to back out of this mess. I tried to move the monster truck as my daughter yelled instructions to turn this way or that. I almost hit a tree, a car, and then both at the same time!

A chivalrous gentleman tried to hide a smile as he asked if we were having problems. He offered his assistance and climbed behind the wheel. Within minutes he had the truck out of the mess I'd created and had it pointing to the street for our escape.

DEVRA'S TIP Make certain you are well rested—spend the money on motels or hotels—and get instructions on how to maneuver the rig you're driving.

Devra also suggests that you ask the rental agency about the equipment you'll be driving. Know how to load, secure, and unload your vehicle from a tow dolly. Here's Devra's "bouncing car" experience:

It was the first day of our moving adventure, and we were excited about getting to our new home. Everything was loaded, including the car being towed on a carrier behind a twenty-foot rental truck. The rental company had been kind enough to load the car and secure it to the trailer. We were set!

We were headed down a steep, windy mountain road when something just didn't feel right with the way the truck was handling. It felt like the car was bouncing behind the rental truck, but we could barely see what was happening to the small SUV in the side mirrors.

Traffic flew by as we tried to hold the truck at sixty-five miles per hour down the grade. I kept saying to my daughter, "I think the car is bouncing."

She disagreed and assured me the car was tied down to the carrier; she'd watched the man secure it. We continued navigating our way down the long hill and noticed that people were flashing their lights and honking as they zipped by us. Obviously, they saw something we couldn't. We decided to pull off the highway to find out why other drivers were trying to get our attention and why the truck felt odd.

We walked around to the trailer and inspected our car. Much to our horror, we discovered the two rear tires were not locked down to the trailer! If the locks on the front tires had not held, the car could have come right off the trailer and into traffic.

We hadn't thoroughly checked to make certain the car was secure and had, instead, relied on the rental company to do it correctly. And we hadn't asked for or been given any instruction on what to do if there was a problem.

We called the rental company, and they agreed to send someone out to remedy the problem. In the meantime, we were stranded, waiting in middle-of-nowhere Arizona in 115-degree heat for over an hour with our dog.

The rest of the trip was a bit intimidating. We constantly checked the SUV on the trailer to make certain it was secure and prayed that it didn't decide to fly off into traffic. The entire event could have been avoided if they had originally done the job properly, if we had verified that it was correctly loaded on the trailer, and if they'd shown us what to do in an emergency.

DEVRA'S TIP Know your equipment and what to do in an emergency. To prevent problems, check and double-check how things are loaded and if they are secured well and locked down before you start your journey. Don't assume. Verify!

Budget for Your Move

It's important to stay within the parameters of a budget. Always set aside extra just-in-case money for unanticipated expenses.

Truck rental	
Trailer rental	

Insurance	
Fuel	
Lodging	
Food	
Car trailer	
Dolly	
Boxes	
Packing materials	
Help	
Just-in-case money	
Total estimate	

Courtesy of 1-800-PACK-RAT, 2021

Container Moving

An excellent option for people who don't want to drive a rental truck is container moving. Convenience is the primary benefit. You reserve a date that the containers are dropped off at your residence and the date they are to be picked up. You pack your belongings into them, and then the company retrieves the loaded container. They either store it until you are ready for it or deliver it to your new address, where you unload it. You are the only one who has a key to lock and unlock the container. You determine how much time you will need to load and unload the container and schedule drop-off times around your needs. An added convenience is that containers have ground-level loading capability, which means you don't have to lug heavy objects up and down ramps. That's a back-saver!

We asked James L. Burati III, Chief Sales Officer of 1-800-PACK-RAT/Zippy Shell, why his company and container moving is becoming so popular. He responded:

> 1-800-PACK-RAT makes moving and storage simple. We provide convenience and flexibility when it comes to moving and storage. We will bring a secure, weatherproof, all-steel portable storage container to your home that you can pack at your pace. When you are ready, we will pick up your container and deliver it to your new home or place it into storage at one of our nationwide warehouse facilities for as long as you need. It is that simple when you work with 1-800-PACK-RAT.[8]

Container moving takes the stress out of maneuvering a large truck to haul your belongings from point A to point B, and delivery and pickup can be scheduled according to your needs. Container services are generally "no-contact" arrangements, which means that you don't have to meet the drivers who deliver and pick up the containers. That helps free up your schedule. And if you run into a delay, most companies will work with you to help make the transition of residences as smooth as possible. If you need to store your belongings for an extended period of time before the final move, there are companies that have storage facilities available. This is ideal if you are military and being stationed overseas or if you don't have a primary residence in the new location yet. You can do a mini-move with essential items, and once you know where your primary residence will be, you can have the container company deliver the remainder of your belongings to your new doorstep. Both 1-800-PACK-RAT and U-Box®, owned by U-Haul®, supply storage services.

Considering fuel prices, containers may be a more economical way to move as well. This is especially true if you're moving across the country. Using a container company means there are fewer unexpected expenses. You select the company, determine the size of the container, agree to the terms, schedule the drop-off and pickup dates, and start packing. If gas prices rise, you're still locked into your original quote, unlike a rental truck, where you're responsible for all fuel costs. You won't have to estimate the drive times in a rental truck, which are not known for being speedy. Nor will you have to check the route for road construction restrictions, available lodging and parking, or any number of potential obstacles involved in a self-move with a rental truck.

Another upside is that there are far fewer property damage claims with container moving as compared to traditional moving companies because you are the only one who touches and packs your belongings. You can take your time to make certain it's done right. Some companies do offer to connect you with professionals who can help you pack and load the containers. The choice is yours. Do you need help, or are you capable of doing it yourself?

Will container moving work for you? Answer yes or no to the following questions:

____ Do I want to drive a rental truck?
____ Do I know how to drive a large truck?
____ Am I on a strict budget?

____ Is time an issue?

____ Do my belongings need to be stored before arrival at my final
location?

If you answered no to two or more of those but still want to move
yourself, you might consider container moving.

Determining the size of the container you need requires estimating
the cubic feet of your belongings. To calculate cubic feet, multiply the
length by the width by the height. If you're calculating space in a container, use the following guide to estimate the container size you need.

8-Foot Container	12-Foot Container	16-Foot Container
Typically holds 1–2 rooms of furniture	Typically holds 2–3 rooms of furniture	Typically holds 3–4 rooms of furniture
About the size of an 8′ x 8′ storage room	About the size of a 10′ x 10′ storage room	About the size of a 10′ x 15′ storage room
Holds up to 4,000 lbs of contents	Holds up to 6,000 lbs of contents	Holds up to 6,000 lbs of contents
404 cubic feet	620 cubic feet	830 cubic feet

Courtesy of 1-800-PACKRAT

Companies offer different sizes of containers, and while some ship
nationally, others are limited to the specific locations they serve. Contact the company you are considering to see if they provide service
in your departure and arrival area. This is a growing industry that's
serving our mobile population, and changes are happening all the time.

Some communities and homeowners associations (HOAs) do not allow containers on roads or on residential property for an extended period of time. Check the regulations in the neighborhood you're leaving and at your new residence. It's important to know the guidelines of your new neighborhood to prevent overstepping their boundaries. If you live in an apartment complex, get permission to bring a container onto the grounds and ask management to help you locate an area where the container can be placed while you load or unload.

If it's going to take more than a day to load the container, you should check with your insurance to make certain that what is loaded into the container is covered. Packing a full house into a container can take a few days, and it's best to make certain your possessions will be insured for loss and damage.

Traditional Moving Companies

If you're moving a houseful of belongings or just want someone else to do all the work, a traditional moving company may be the best option, especially if there is a long distance between the old and new residences. There are companies that will load and move and unload what you've packed. And there are companies that are full-service and will come to your house, pack your belongings, and relocate them to your new home. In some cases, they will also unpack your boxes for you.

Once you make the decision to use a traditional moving company, the next step is to select a reputable company. You can find a list of the top moving companies in the resources at the back of this book. Spend some time on the internet reading about the services provided by different moving lines. Then perhaps ask relatives, neighbors, friends, and social media acquaintances for references on companies you've researched. People will scream loudly about unscrupulous companies. Plan to get a minimum of three bids, compare the costs of all the services they offer, and check each company with the Better Business Bureau (BBB). Ask the moving companies if they have any unsettled disputes and how they settle differences. You have the right to know that, and the methods of remedy should be in their customer agreement.

It's up to you to thoroughly read and fully understand the contract and know which solutions are available to you in the event there are problems. If you have a question, pose it. Don't be shy. You are entrusting your property to someone else, and you have a right to know the company's policies and practices.

Pricing differs greatly in what moving companies consider on- and off-season. This is true of small and large, local and national companies. If you can be flexible about the time of year you move, you might save 30 percent or more during the company's specified off-season. Companies have different dates in which their seasons begin and end. If you're too close to their on-season date, you may be stuck with the higher rate.

What to Watch Out For

Be aware that there are a few disreputable companies with websites and names that are intentionally similar to the better-known businesses. Sometimes the websites and names are so similar, people mistake them for the real deal.

When you research companies online, don't put your personal information into a "free quote estimate." The response back is usually from an agent representing hundreds of companies. Some of those companies may not be reputable. The agent gets a commission from every move they book, and no matter what they promise or what prices they quote, the moving company is not obligated to stand by that representative's statement.

When reviewing a moving company's website, note the address, phone number, and email address. If they don't list those, keep looking. Avoid providing them with your personal or credit card information until you have thoroughly vetted them. Some scams have included ID theft from moving ads run in local papers or on websites.

Professional movers should be able to provide the name of their insurance company and the number of the policy. Verify the information. Consider that part of your responsibility, as well as making certain that the interstate-moving company you're considering is registered with the Federal Motor Carrier Safety Association (FMCSA) and the United States Department of Transportation (USDOT). A reputable mover should have no problem supplying that information.

Once you determine the top three companies that you're interested in dealing with, get estimates. Be explicit about the services you require and the pickup and arrival dates for your belongings. Read the contract and ask questions. What happens if the moving van is delayed and they don't meet the guaranteed delivery date? What happens if the delivery arrives before you do? What happens if items are missing or damaged?

A bid should not bind you to an agreement.

The most accurate estimates are made when someone from the company comes to your home, looks at everything to be moved, and gives you a written estimate. If they attempt to quote a fee by phone, request an on-site review. An estimate made over the phone and sight unseen is not binding. The difference in the actual cost could tank your budget.

Most reputable firms send licensed representatives to your home to create a written estimate. The estimate—and the final agreement—should give you a guarantee that, once the truck is fully loaded, the final price will not go more than 10 percent above the estimated price. If they don't do this and the guarantee is not written into the contract, then it's best not to choose them as your movers.

Unfortunately, there are a number of scams out there. One is that a company gives you a non-written quote, collects the deposit, and loads their truck, only to disappear with your belongings. Be cautious of requests for large deposits or even payment in full before the move. You will always pay a deposit, but ethical companies will have the driver pick up the final payment when your shipment arrives and is unloaded at its destination.

Recently, people have complained that they've arrived at their new residence only to find their belongings are being held hostage by movers who are demanding more money than the client agreed to. If you don't have a signed a contract with a written estimate, a mover *can* hold your property hostage. That's why it's important the contract states payment in full will not exceed a percentage of the agreed-upon estimate.

Movers aren't allowed to hold your things hostage if you've paid 100 percent of the estimated costs outlined on your binding estimate, or 110 percent of the estimated costs on your non-binding estimate, or have met the required deposit agreement. Review your paperwork; know what you are signing.

Get everything in writing! Countering a verbal discussion or agreement is almost impossible. If it's not in writing, you're at their mercy.

DEVRA'S TIP If you don't know the exact date the moving van will arrive, pack your car as though you might have to live without your other furnishings for a while. A suitcase with personal items and clothes, an air mattress or sleeping bag, and maybe a coffee maker, cups, silverware, paper plates, and paper towels will help you manage a couple of days of camping in your new home.

Short-Distance Moving and Local Companies

If you're moving across town, you might consider hiring a local moving company. There are local movers in just about every town. These smaller companies provide a variety of options for your move and are worth looking into. If you are in a college town, there may be entrepreneurial students who can be hired to do the heavy lifting if you rent the truck. When it comes to finding local moving companies, references from friends and family are the most reliable. The Better Business Bureau (BBB) and social media can help too.

Most local businesses charge by the hour, but they're usually fast and efficient when loading and unloading. It's to your advantage to have everything packed and wrapped and ready to load when they arrive at your door.

Devra recalls a happy local move:

I'd heard about a local company with a funny name: Two Men and a Truck. After doing my research, speaking with them, and getting a bid, I decided to hire them. When they arrived, they put down runners to protect the carpet and taped pads on walls and staircases to prevent damage.

They billed by the hour, but these guys didn't dawdle. They had estimated three hours to load, and they worked without a break to meet that time.

They took such care loading and unloading my possessions, which they did in record time, and were professional and courteous.

It is so nice when you find people who care about their work and their clients the way this company did. I used them three times, and every experience had the same high-quality care.

DEVRA'S TIP There are many local companies like this out there. Do your homework, get feedback from others who have used their services, make sure the company is bonded and insured, and find one that fits your needs.

Before signing anything, verify as much as you can about the company. Ask for their insurance company's name. Make sure they are insured for any damages to your property. If they aren't insured and bonded, don't sign a contract. Check their reputation via references and the Better Business Bureau. Read the agreement thoroughly and be certain of what elements of a move it covers and doesn't cover.

Things to Keep in Mind

Pickup and Delivery

Give yourself ample time for both pickup and delivery. Movers may only guarantee a three-day window for pickup, with twenty-four-hour notice, and delivery will vary. It might be as long as twenty-one days from the date of pickup. Drivers may be hauling other loads going to different states, and they don't like to come back with an empty truck. Your possessions may have quite a road trip before they arrive at your new residence.

Partial Loads

If your possessions don't fill a moving van, you will still have to pay the minimum weight price, and your load may be mixed in with other shipments that might be delivered before yours.

Price by the Foot

Movers who price by the square foot instead of by the cubic foot, weight, and distance might be less expensive, providing your packed and loaded belongings don't exceed the estimated footage. You, or someone you trust, must be present to make sure the space is used efficiently so your property doesn't exceed the estimate.

Devra learned a costly lesson with a price-by-the-foot move.

On a move from San Diego to Arizona, I thought I would try a new company that I'd found online that priced by the foot. The woman I spoke with seemed nice and knowledgeable, and the company had a good rating with the Better Business Bureau. I decided to go forward with what I thought was a well-researched option with a reputable company. The price was estimated by phone and was based on all my boxes and furniture and what square footage would be used in the truck.

All was fine the day of the move. The loaders were polite and careful with my stuff. It wasn't until they got the truck completely packed that the driver informed me that I had gone so many feet over the estimate that I owed him an additional one thousand dollars. When I told him that I did not have an additional thousand dollars, he informed me that they had the right to hold my belongings hostage and charge me by the day for storage until I came up with the money I owed, as well as the money for storage. When I told the driver that the person on the phone had told me it was guaranteed not to be more than 10 percent of the estimate, he informed me that the person I was talking to was an independent contractor who did bookings for several companies and could not promise any particular fee.

I had no option. I was ready to go to our new home in Arizona with my daughter, my granddaughter, two dogs, and a cat waiting on the curb. I wrote him a check for the thousand dollars and chalked this up to yet one more expensive moving lesson.

 DEVRA'S TIP Do your due diligence! Check multiple sources for references. Don't jump at the promise of something that sounds too good to be true.

Preparing for the Move

Create an inventory of items you're moving. The movers will give you a copy of their inventory, but this is a backup for you. Taking pictures or videos of your furnishings before the move is a great way to keep track of your possessions. Images are also good to have should any damage occur and you need to prove that dents, scratches, or broken objects were the result of the move.

How to Transport Your Vehicle(s)

If you hired movers, you might simply be driving to your new location. If you're self-moving, you may choose to tow your vehicle behind a rental truck. But if you aren't driving to your new location or you have more than one vehicle, you might need an auto-moving company. You can find reputable car transport companies through local auto dealerships, who use the companies to deliver vehicles from auctions and other dealerships.

There are a few auto-moving businesses that provide door-to-door service, but they're expensive. It's perfect if you have a high-end or classic car, but that's not financially feasible for most people. If you have a very valuable vehicle, companies will ship it in an enclosed carrier.

Commonly, the carrier will want to meet you at a nearby location, preferably right off the freeway. Truck stops and rest areas are usually suggested, as this lets the driver, who will load and unload your vehicle(s), be on their way.

Have copies of your vehicle's registration and insurance papers, a picture of the license plate, and pictures or videos of the interior and exterior of the vehicle before your car is loaded on the trailer. This is proof of the condition of the vehicle prior to it being transported. When it's delivered, if there are new dents, scratches, or worn paint from straps that weren't secured properly, you have proof that it did not leave in that condition.

Place a photograph of the car with the owner's cell phone number inside the car, against the front windshield on the driver's side. If there is a problem or the carrier needs to contact you about delivery, your information is readily available.

Get bids and vet auto-moving companies as you did with other companies. You don't want your vehicle to end up in a chop shop. Hiring an individual to drive your car might be less expensive, but you might be liable for damages, should any occur. Check your insurance, which should remain active and current, no matter how your vehicle is moved.

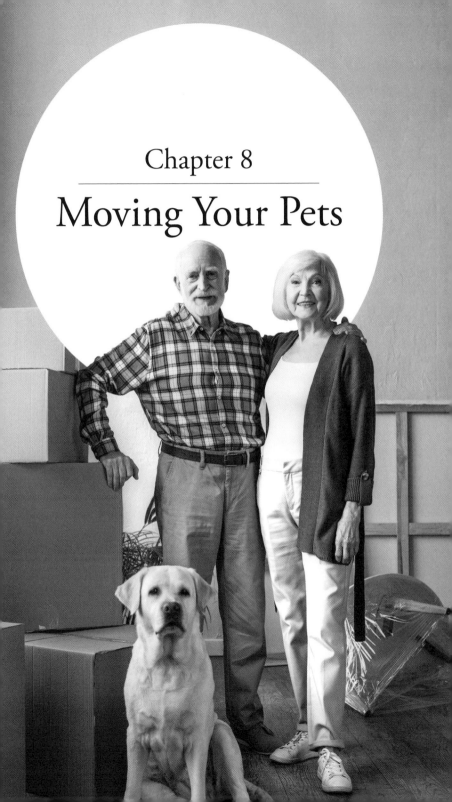

Chapter 8
Moving Your Pets

I f you will be driving to your new home and making overnight stops along the way, it's wise to make reservations with places that accept pets.

If you have a certified service animal and are flying to your destination, check with the airline to see if your animal is acceptable. Some species are no longer considered acceptable service animals, and there may be size issues. Airlines are generally good about explaining their policies, and it's important to have this information before you plan your flight.

If you don't want to travel with your pets, there are other ways to transport them to your new location. Companies offer services that will move your furry family members via vehicle or air. Get online and research "pet transportation services" to see what is available in your area.

Managing the departure and arrival times of your animals is key to successful pet transportation. Someone will need to be present when the pet is picked up and, at the other end of the journey, when they arrive.

Different types and breeds of animals have different needs. Are there special health considerations? Is your pet a six-week-old puppy or very old? Does it require medication on a regular schedule? Is it "snub nosed"—called brachycephalic—like a bulldog or Persian cat, or overweight? If so, will your pet have difficulty breathing on an airplane? Will your pet be able to handle extreme temperatures? How do they feel about strangers caring for them? Do you have a nontraditional pet like a reptile or farm animal? Questions like these need to be thoroughly explored with a pet transportation business.

Immunizations must be up-to-date, and you may need a release from your vet, especially if the animal is being shipped by air. You will need to provide a copy of the pet's health records and, in some cases, special permits may be needed. The transport company can help you with that.

If Hawaii or Guam is your final destination, visit their animal quarantine page to get the latest information. If you are moving out of the country, the pet transportation company will be able to guide you through the paperwork and quarantine information.

Should you be deployed for the military, you may not be able take your furry friend with you. But there are organizations that will care for your pet while you're in service. These groups provide peace of mind for military personnel during their service commitments because they provide long-term boarding or, in some cases, find foster homes for your pet. This is a wonderful asset when family and friends are unable to assist in caring for pets during a military deployment.

If you're traveling with your furry family members, you will need a carrier or a seat safety harness. Traveling can cause stress in animals; some even get carsick. Keep them as calm as possible. It's wise to have a pet-friendly calmative, which is available over the counter, or an anti-anxiety medication suggested by your veterinarian. Keep them hydrated; offer water whenever you stop. Be prepared for plenty of potty stops, and don't forget playtime! Neither animals nor humans are designed to be in a vehicle for long stretches of time. Your beloved pets need to move and stretch, and so do you!

Throughout the years, Devra has moved with many types of pets.

Moving with pets can be interesting, to say the least. And, depending on what kinds of pets you own, research is very important. We have always loved animals, so our moves have included cats, dogs, a rabbit, a lizard, and fish.

On my first move in a car with my cat, I quickly learned that you might need tranquilizers for the animal. As soon as I started driving, my poor cat pinned itself to a window, paws sprawled out like a Garfield window sticker, and she started talking . . . *Meow, meow, meow, let me out of here!*

I was lucky that this move was just a few hours away, or we both would have lost our minds.

My advice is to make an appointment with your vet well before a move to get kitty or puppy tranquilizers, for the sanity of both you and your pet.

We moved with a rabbit once, which meant buying a small carrier. It needed to be just large enough for the bunny to turn around, because if it were any larger, the bunny would run itself in circles, could get injured, and might suffer even more stress. We gave the bunny a test-drive to see how he would do, and he wasn't thrilled with the sounds and motions of the car. Due to his small size, tranquilizers were not going to be possible, but the vet recommended Rescue Remedy Pet to keep him calm during the hours in the car. It worked wonderfully. He stayed calm through the entire trip.

Our latest move was the most interesting. It included three people, two dogs, and a panther chameleon that was fourteen inches long. We knew we would be on the road for at least two days on the journey from Northern California to Arizona, and it was the beginning of summer. Why was the time of year important? Well, it turns out that this lizard cannot get hotter than eighty degrees. Stopping for potty breaks or to stretch meant leaving the car and air-conditioning running. It was impossible to stop at a diner for a relaxing meal, so we learned the location of every drive-thru restaurant off Interstates 5 and 40.

This kind of lizard is surprisingly easy to travel with other than the regulated temperatures. Panthers, when placed in a dark box, will simply go to sleep until you take them back out. It is not recommended that you do this for more than a couple of days. When you stop at a hotel for the night, you do not need to remove them from the box. Wedge a perch between the sides of the box, so that it has something to grip, and use a towel to cushion the bottom of the box in case it falls off the perch. Our lizard arrived at its new home in good health and happy to wake back up.

Your unique pet may require specific travel conditions. Be certain to see to their needs for health and safety.

DEVRA'S TIP No matter the type of pet you will be moving with, do your research. Pets can also get carsick. Take them for a drive before you start out on the road and see how they react. Will they need a calmative? Do they throw up after a few minutes? If they do have a sensitive tummy, avoid feeding them or giving them too much water before you start out. They will need water throughout the trip but not a great deal at one time. Calmatives can help with carsickness, and there are also motion sickness medications you can get from the veterinarian.

The resources section at the back of this book provides some more valuable information.

Chapter 9

Now for the Physical Work

A happy move is so well organized that you don't feel overwhelmed in the process. Moving can cause stress. Organizing the move will help alleviate anxiety.

Making some judgment calls about what you are taking with you is important. Moving is a great way to clean closets and drawers. Set aside clothes that no longer fit you or members of your family for donation. Do the same for toys, games, and books: if they are no longer of interest to you or your family, give them away. Someone will appreciate them. You can sell lightly used and unwanted furniture and appliances. These are all good tips to keep in mind, especially if you are downsizing.

Packing

One of the most important parts of any move is packing. What you take, how you put it in boxes, and how it's identified can make arrival at your new home a joy or a nightmare.

Packing your own belongings, even if you are using a large, professional company for the actual move, is helpful on many levels. First, it generally saves you money. Second, you can organize boxes by room and contents. Third, you can clearly mark the box with the location and contents so that when you begin unpacking, you know exactly where things go. It's disheartening to unpack a box labeled "Kitchen" to find it's full of laundry room supplies that go on the other side of the house. There's no sense in creating extra work; organization helps prevent that.

Devra recalls a move made by her parents:

My parents thought it would be much easier to have the professionals pack for them. But what they didn't realize was that these people would pack anything they got their hands on in the same box. It didn't matter what room it came from or if they put a toilet plunger in with the toaster. When we unloaded the boxes, we found things like plant pots that still had old dirt in them, which created extra weight and quite a mess in the boxes. One box labeled "Misc. Bedroom" had broken perfume bottles that had been packed with shoes and purses, which were odoriferous to say the least. Every purse and all the shoes that were in that box had to be thrown away.

DEVRA'S TIP When you can't pack it yourself, oversee the work of others. Make requests and speak up when you see something you question or dislike. These are your possessions, and you want them to arrive in good condition.

There are certain items that go hand in hand with any type of move: boxes; tape; some type of cushioning like bubble wrap, paper, or packing popcorn; and markers. They are absolutely necessary to ensure your property arrives safely and undamaged. Having the right tools will make packing easier and unpacking more efficient.

Boxes

Grabbing boxes from behind the local grocer might seem like a bright idea because it's easy and less expensive. But packing in used boxes usually is an example of the old adage "penny smart, pound foolish."

You can buy inexpensive new boxes from an office supply store, hardware store, storage facility, or rental truck store. That ensures that nothing else has been in that box prior to your possessions. And you don't want to give critters like roaches, spiders, and ants a free ride to your new location. New boxes are clean and bug-free.

U-Haul® told us about their eco-friendly boxes:

> If you are making an in-town move, consider renting eco-friendly, plastic, U-Haul Ready-To-Go® Boxes that can be returned to your local U-Haul® store upon unpacking. Otherwise, take comfort in knowing that any unused cardboard boxes you purchase from uhaul.com or a U-Haul® rental location can be returned for a full refund with your U-Haul® receipt.[9]

The essential reason for purchasing or renting boxes is that you can ensure consistent sizes and shapes, which will let you stack them properly in the truck, thus preventing crushing and unnecessary damage.

You'll probably need small, medium, and large boxes. If you keep the dimensions uniform, they will stack better in the truck or container. Some people like to use cell dividers within a box for glasses and other fragile items. They can be helpful, and you might want to purchase some where you buy your boxes.

Small boxes are good for packing heavy items like silverware, dishes, cups, glasses, books, and file folders. They are ideal for small, well-wrapped, breakable collectibles. Items from the pantry like dried beans and canned goods fit well in a small box. If you have a rock collection, use a small box to transport your treasures. The objective is to avoid making a box too heavy to lift.

Medium-sized boxes work well for clothes, shoes, lampshades, and knickknacks.

Large boxes are ideal for lamps and other large or oddly shaped items that require additional room for the packing materials you'll secure around them. They're great for a stuffed animal collection and the contents of your linen closet. Anything that has an unusual form like oddly shaped cake pans or extra-large cookie sheets should go in a large box.

A wardrobe box can pull double duty. It's perfect for clothes because it comes with a metal bar for hanging, but it is also great for brooms, mops, and upright vacuum cleaners. When packing tall, fragile items, like a floor lamp, hang clothes on either side of it for extra padding.

Flat-screen televisions and computer monitors require a special box. These are pricy possessions that you don't want to have to replace. A specialized container made of heavier cardboard, with foam corners, is good to move them. The only thing better is the original box, which you should use if you have it.

There are other specialized boxes designed to protect artwork, including paintings and sculptures. Pack these valuable items very carefully to ensure their safe transport. A properly sized box is worth the cost, as these items cannot be replaced.

Devra learned the value of having everything in a box when one item was lost and another gained:

I had an old upright vacuum cleaner that didn't really have any value. It would not fit inside any of the boxes I had, so it went onto the moving truck with just a little sticker that identified it as mine. The driver put the sticker on so he'd know where to leave it. Somehow it never came out of the truck on the other end of the move. Instead, I was given a cool little three-step step stool.

I notified the driver immediately that it was not my step stool and that I was missing an upright vacuum. The driver smiled and said, "Well, I've done five deliveries over the last three weeks, and I have no idea who owns the step stool. You're welcome to keep it if you like. As for the vacuum, turn in a lost item report to the moving company to have it replaced at current market value."

I chose to simply keep the step stool, and to my surprise, it was one of the best household items I've owned. It's survived fifteen moves since then, but now I always move it in a tall wardrobe box with my mops, brooms, and vacuum cleaners so nobody else ends up with my wonderful little step stool.

DEVRA'S TIP Pack everything in boxes to prevent losing loose items. To build a sturdy box, fold the bottom flaps to create the base. Then tape the box in both directions, top to bottom and side to side, for extra support across the bottom. When sealing the box on top, you can use a single section of tape along the seam where the flaps come together. And keep a knife or scissors handy in case you have to open a box that's sealed.

Packing Materials

Bubble wrap and packing paper or butcher paper are indispensable. Rolls or sheets of packing paper are necessary because it's hard to find old newspapers these days. Also, the downside of using newsprint is that not only will it leave your fingertips black but it can discolor items you're wrapping in it, which means extra cleaning when you arrive and unpack. Packing paper is relatively inexpensive and can be purchased at a hardware store or truck rental company. It can also be recycled.

As insignificant or obvious as it sounds, packing tape is another crucial ingredient to a happy move. Clear, two-inch wide packing tape with a dispenser is best. The dispenser will make life much easier because you won't be searching for scissors or a knife or getting frustrated when the end of the tape sticks to the roll and you have to peel it off. Brown paper packing tape isn't efficient because the slightest bit of moisture will cause it to either pull loose from the box or tear. You don't want the irritation of picking up a box only to have everything fall out of the bottom.

Set aside towels, blankets, and sheets, as they are some of the best packing materials you will use. T-shirts, sweatpants, or sweatshirts and seasonal clothing are also wonderful to wrap items in or to pad the bottom of a box. Using items like these for cushioning and packing is economical. You won't have to purchase extra bubble wrap, which makes it better for the environment too.

If you don't have any extra blankets, you can rent them from a truck rental agency or container company. These are important because they help protect your furniture from scratches.

Get wide, black, felt-tip markers for identifying the room and contents of each box. Always mark the boxes on the top and at least one side. By marking them on the top, you know which way is up and which way is down. The side marking is to identify what room the box goes to whether it is delivered to that room or stacked in the living room first.

What Should You Pack First?

Think about the things in your house that are rarely used. When was the last time you used the punch bowl stashed behind the mixing bowls? Are you likely to use it before you move? If not, pack it with all other nonessential kitchen items. As you position things in the boxes, realize that most damage is from the up and down and side to side motion or vibrations in a truck. Pack accordingly to protect your treasures.

The amount of time needed to pack is up to you and your schedule. Some people prefer to pack a little each day over a longer period of time, and there are others who want to box up an entire household in three days or less. Do what is best for you, your schedule, your lifestyle, and your peace of mind, but don't procrastinate.

The Kitchen

First, pack small kitchen appliances or kitchenware that you rarely use. Good china, serving dishes, and cookbooks can also be packed first. Put the heavier items on the bottom of the box and build up. Keep the weight manageable. If the box is too heavy, you might strain your back.

In Storage

Holiday decorations should also be packed early on in the process. You may already have decorations packed in boxes or plastic storage containers. Be sure they are packed full but are not too heavy to carry.

The Bedroom

Hats, shoes, belts, and other accessories that you're not going to wear can be packed early. Use throw pillows to cushion the bottom and sides of boxes that will hold fragile items such as figurines and knickknacks. Off-season clothing works well as padding in boxes too.

The Living/Family Room

Room decorations, accent mirrors, curios, and books can be packed early. DVDs, tablets, games, toys, CDs, and books are good ways to keep children occupied on a long drive or while you are busy packing or unpacking. Set aside their favorites but pack away others that won't be used. Use small boxes for books, to control the weight.

The Backyard

Toys and bird feeders should be cleaned well and then wrapped and packed. A gas BBQ should be scrubbed clean. Remove the propane tank from a gas grill. It's not recommended that you carry propane tanks inside your personal vehicle, and some moving companies refuse to transport them. If you must bring it along, place it in an upright position and secure it. Never leave propane tanks in a hot car, as they can explode. The best thing to do is to return them to the store from which they were purchased. There are other places, including some gas stations, that will take a used tank off your hands. Once you have determined the fate of the propane tank, wrap the grill in plastic wrap, often called pallet wrap, that can be bought in large rolls at the hardware store. Then cover and cushion it with an old blanket.

DEVRA'S TIPS

- Dust items before packing them. This will save you a lot of work when you arrive.
- Bottles that contain liquid should be sealed in a plastic bag, in case the lid leaks. This will prevent spills or leaks onto other items.
- To help secure liquid or cream contents, you can also remove the lid, place plastic wrap over the top, and replace the lid tightly before placing it in a sealable plastic bag.
- Paperwork, such as past taxes or legal papers, and family photos should be copied and stored on a digital device. Place the hard copies in waterproof plastic containers of a manageable size. Mark each container, noting the contents. The waterproof box with legal papers should travel with you and not with the container or moving company.
- Plan on using up food and cleaning supplies before the move so that you don't feel like you have to lug them with you. No one likes to waste anything; using these things will help you feel like you're making headway.
- Think about what's going into each box. Separate items that might contaminate each other.

The Bathroom

The bathroom is one of the last rooms to be packed. Place anything that might spill in a sealed plastic bag before wrapping it and placing it in the box. Separate frequently used medications and prescriptions so that you can keep them with you while traveling. All others can be packed and clearly labeled.

Packing Tips

Proper packing decreases the chance of damage and allows you to fit more into a specific space.

When packing a box, place heavy items on the bottom. Before you pack anything breakable, pad the bottom of the box with a towel or sheet so the item will not be damaged. Add items that are lighter until the box is completely filled. Always fill the box all the way to the top to prevent crushing the cardboard and damaging the contents during the move.

Wrap fragile items such as glassware, picture frames, and small knickknacks in bubble wrap, clothing, or paper and then wrap them again in either a pillowcase or T-shirt for extra padding.

In the resources at the back of this book, there are links to videos demonstrating Devra's packing tips.

Think Ahead

You've arrived at your new home, boxes are stacked everywhere, and all you want to do is sit down and have a cup of coffee. You look around. You know the coffeepot was packed in a medium box, but none of them are marked.

Twenty boxes later, you find the coffeepot. But then you wonder where you packed the coffee!

That's the type of scenario you can expect if you haven't identified the room the box belongs in and its contents. This type of thing happens to most people, but there's a simple solution: A thick felt pen does the trick. As soon as you tape a box closed, mark it!

Make a note on the box of the contents and the room they came from. An example is "Timmy's Room—pj's, games, stuffed animals." When your family is ready for the first night in the new home, you know little Timmy will have the calming comfort of familiar items to help him sleep.

If you're making a long-distance move, you'll have your personal necessities and extra clothes in a suitcase that travels with you, but some things in the truck will be needed for immediate use when they arrive at their final destination, making organization extra important.

Devra learned the value of labeling boxes the hard way:

We had just moved, and I was trying to get my daughter registered at the new school. I didn't realize that beyond the normal vaccination and medical history, you had to have a birth certificate as well as the child custody agreement or divorce settlement.

I had very carefully packed all our important documents in a box for the move, but all those carefully packed unlabeled boxes were stacked all over the new apartment, and they all looked alike! It took me two weeks to find the documents I needed, which meant she started the new semester late and was two weeks behind the other students.

In retrospect, this could have easily been avoided if I had just known to make a phone call to the school prior to the move and had clearly marked each box so that the contents were obvious.

DEVRA'S TIP Think ahead and label your boxes.

Pack two boxes with essentials that you'll need the day you arrive. Even if you plan to eat out the first day or two, having these items will help you feel more at home. The first box should contain kitchen essentials like a dish/hand towel, salt and pepper, paper plates, disposable cups and flatware (or camping utensils), dish soap, and the coffee maker and coffee (or the teakettle and tea). The second box should contain cleaning and bathroom essentials like paper towels, toilet paper, an all-purpose cleaner, a roll of garbage bags, hand sanitizer, soap, and other hygiene products like body soap and shampoo. Mark the boxes boldly: "Open first."

For Fellow Control Freaks

Inventory your furniture. You can make lists on the lined pages starting on page 221 of every piece of furniture that is loaded on the truck. For example, "Living Room: Couch, loveseat, chair, end tables (2), coffee table, entertainment center, curio cabinet." Photograph these items prior to prepping them for the truck. This way you know exactly what is to be loaded and what condition it was in before the move.

There are those who want an extremely organized transition of homes. We recommend they pick up a spiral notebook, thoroughly inventory the contents of each box as it's being packed, and note if it was loaded on the truck. Most of us are fine simply identifying the room and contents on the box, but some find that a more detailed method works best for them. Here's an example:

Room ID	Box ID	Contents	Loaded (Y/N)
Bedroom 1	1	Sweaters, hats, socks	Y
Bedroom 1	2	Underwear, trinkets, scarves	Y
Bedroom 2	1	Puzzles, toys, kids' books	

You may have twelve boxes for bedroom one and nine for bedroom two. By using this inventory system, you'll know what's in each box, if it was loaded on the truck, and which box you want to unpack first. It is extra work, but it's a method that some people prefer.

Things to Never Pack or Ship

There are certain possessions that should never be packed and placed in a truck, container, or moving van.

Don't identify valuable contents that might be of interest to someone unscrupulous by labeling them on the box. Avoid bringing attention to collectibles, jewelry boxes, artwork, or anything else of extreme value. The movers or helpers may be nice people, but it's best not to give someone an opportunity to succumb to temptation.

Keep valuable jewelry in a box that will travel with you. Don't mark the box as anything valuable because you don't want to risk anything being stolen. Identify the box with general terms like kitchen/food or bedroom/games. Or your family can come up with a covert name to mark boxes containing valuables.

Personal belongings like address books, checkbooks, keys, medicine, and school, tax, and legal records should not be put on a truck. Those should be with you at all times during the move.

Caustic items such as insecticides, fertilizers, weed killers, and household cleaners should never be packed for shipment to your new home. There are substances moving companies do not allow on a moving truck. Never pack combustible items like gasoline, paint thinner, motor oil, propane, lighter fluid, or aerosols. Explosives such as ammunition and fireworks also fall into the never-pack-or-ship category. The same is true of car batteries, nail polish remover, and any corrosive material or liquid. Check to see if your community has a hazardous waste collection point, or check with friends and neighbors to see if they might have a use for these materials. Many of them cannot go in the trash and should never be poured down the drain.

Don't bring perishable foods on your move. If you can't eat it before you leave, give it to a neighbor or friend.

How to Fill That Box

Now that you've determined what your packing priorities are, you need the pack items properly. The following are some specific methods of packing that are helpful and will protect your possessions.

Packing Glasses

Always pack glasses vertically. When they're laid on their sides, the friction in the box can cause cracking. To wrap them, set your paper down with the glass lying horizontally on top and start rolling from one corner. Fold the paper into the top of the glass and keep rolling until the glass is completely wrapped. Folding the paper into the top of each glass will lessen vibration in the box. Use bubble wrap or packing paper to fill vacant areas inside and between the glasses. If you buy a box with cardboard separators or cells, still wrap each glass before inserting it in the cell. You don't want them rattling around in the box.

There are two ways to protect your stemware such as wineglasses and champagne flutes. One way is to fill the interior of two glasses with packing paper. Then roll one glass in about half the length of packing paper. Place another glass next to the wrapped glass with the top of one next to the bottom of the other. Continue tightly wrapping the pair in the paper. Fold the ends of the paper over and wrap the pair in another sheet of paper. Place them vertically in a padded box.

The other way is using cell dividers in the box. Fill the interior of the glass with packing paper. Place one glass in each cell, rim-side down, and support the stem of the glass with extra paper.

Plates and Bowls

Completely wrap each plate and bowl in a single layer of paper. If you just put a piece of paper between plates, you won't have enough padding and the edges can chip. Wrap bowls and then stack them inside each other. Keep plates flat and put bowls in around them. Finish packing the box with something light like empty plastic containers. They won't break but will create a strong barrier for the top of the box. If you have glass mixing bowls, you can wrap them one at a time and put them inside plastic bowls or containers for extra protection.

Utensils

Use a plastic container or a shoebox to hold knives, scissors, and other sharp objects to avoid being stabbed when you're unpacking. Pad the sharp objects with paper towels on top. Seal the plastic container and place it into a box. It's not necessary to individually wrap knives when they are packed this way. For convenience, you could do the same with your forks, butter knives, and spoons, as well as any other cooking utensils. Things like wooden spoons and plastic utensils are great to shove into corners of boxes. They take up space that is otherwise unusable and are out of the way.

Small Kitchen Appliances

All kitchen appliances like microwave ovens, air fryers, food processors, and coffee makers should be packed in boxes and labeled accordingly. If the cord is removable, place it inside the appliance or put it in a plastic bag and tape it to the back of the appliance. Avoid the frustration of finding a detached cord and not knowing what it goes to.

Breakable Objects

Wrap each piece with bubble wrap or a piece of clothing and then wrap the cushioned item in a sheet of packing paper. Pad the bottom of the box with a towel or article of clothing. As you place the pieces in the box, stuff socks or T-shirts in between them for extra padding. You can always get more boxes, but you probably won't be able to replace your grandmother's china doll.

Miscellaneous Small Items

Any tiny items like refrigerator magnets should be wrapped in paper and placed into a plastic food container or plastic bag. Keep them together and pack them in a room-appropriate box. That prevents them from being lost or accidently thrown away.

Pictures

Wrap pictures in bubble wrap or clothing and then stack them horizontally. Larger frames go on the bottom, with padding underneath. Then scale down by placing sequentially smaller frames on top. Add padding tightly on the sides to minimize vibration. You can place cardboard pieces between each frame to better cushion the contents of the box. Don't place loose pictures or paintings in plastic, because they can be ruined if there is any humidity during their journey.

Flat-Screen Televisions and Computer Monitors

Only pack flat-screens in vertical boxes made for televisions. If you don't have the original box, buy one to fit the screen. Place the TV in the box and use bedding or towels to gently fill any empty space. This will ensure that there is ample padding to protect your investment.

Large posters or unframed art prints can go in with your TV. Simply slide them between the padding and the inside of the box.

There are two methods of packing remote controls for televisions, stereos, and streaming devices. Remove the batteries and put them in a plastic bag and then wrap the remote and place it in the box with the item it operates. By removing the batteries, you are extending the life of the battery as well as avoiding possible leaking or rupture inside the remote control.

The other way is to gather all remote controls, remove the batteries, and place the controllers individually in plastic bags. The batteries can go in a separate bag. Use a Sharpie to identify on the bag which device the remote is associated with. Wrap each bag in paper or bubble wrap and place all remote controls together, along with the bag of batteries, in a box. Label it "Remote Controls." With either of these two methods, you won't have to unpack every box to find the remote, and you'll be less likely to accidently toss one out.

Lamps and Lampshades

Remove the light bulb, lampshade, and its holder. Pad the bottom of the box. Coil the electric cord around the lamp. Wrap the lamp in bubble wrap and place it in the box. If you have two lamps, they can be packed in the same box. Stuff pillows around the inside edge of the box and use packing paper or bubble wrap to separate the lamps and cushion them so that they don't rub against each other. Use pillows, towels, or bedding to cover the tops of the lamps and fill the box. Secure the box with tape and label it.

You can pack floor lamps in tall wardrobe boxes or specially designed lamp boxes. Wrap and secure them the same way you would handle a table lamp.

Standard lampshades are best loaded upside down in a padded box. You can stack same-sized shades, nested together. Use packing paper to protect the sides of the shades and support them. Make certain they are secure in the box.

Use wadded paper to support the insides of the lampshades. Place the lampshade holders in a plastic baggie; wrap the baggie in packing paper and set it in the center of the lampshade. Wrap up light bulbs, put them in a small plastic container, and place the container inside the lampshade. Fill the box with padding and then tape and label it.

Glass shades or Tiffany-style shades are very fragile. Pad the bottom of a box with a pillow or towel, topped with packing paper that will fill the sides of the box. Wrap a Tiffany-style glass lampshade in a couple of layers of bubble wrap and secure it with tape. Fill the interior of the lampshade with bubble wrap and wrap the entire shade in pallet wrap. Tape that securely in place. You might want to wrap cardboard around the outside of the bubble-wrapped lamp as added protection.

Position the lampshade right side up in the box and fill the interior with bubble wrap and packing paper. Be sure to fill the box completely with packing material to secure the lampshade in place. Tape the box shut, mark the side of the box with an up arrow, and note in big, bold writing, "This side up—FRAGILE."

Furniture

Furniture takes up a lot of room in the truck, and much of it is empty space that could otherwise be used. Breaking furniture down into pieces allows you to use space more efficiently. If your tables have removable legs, take them off. Disassemble any other furnishings like bed frames to make loading and stacking easier. Place any hardware in a plastic bag and tape it securely to the item it came from.

Disassemble bookcases so they won't break and can be easily loaded in the truck. Put the hardware in a plastic bag and securely tape it to one of the pieces of the bookcase. The loose shelves should be wrapped together with plastic wrap. This will prevent confusion when you reassemble the items in your new home.

Remove drawer pulls and handles from chests and armoires and reattach them on the inside of the drawers or put the hardware in plastic bags and tape them inside a drawer of the unit. This prevents loss and damage to the handles or other furnishings.

If you're using a professional moving company, pack the contents of drawers into a box. Leaving contents in the drawers adds to the weight of the object. If you're self-moving and can maneuver the few extra pounds, you can leave clothes in drawers.

Use plastic wrap to cover furniture such as chairs, tables, and dressers. If the furniture scratches easily, cushion it with a blanket and then wrap each item tightly in plastic. As it is loaded in the truck, container, or moving van, each piece of furniture should be covered and cushioned by a blanket. This prevents the surfaces from being scratched in transit. For a self-move, you might need to rent furniture blankets from a rental center.

Rugs

First make sure your rugs are properly cleaned. Then roll them up and secure them in plastic wrap. Roll the rug with the topside facing out. This prevents damage and strain on a rug's backing. Once you've rolled the rug and wrapped it in plastic, tie or tape it securely.

Indoor Houseplants

In most cases you can personally transport houseplants from state to state if they are free of insects and in a commercially prepared soil. Moving companies usually do not transport live plants because they cannot be responsible for a living thing on their truck for days or a week or more. You need to move them in your vehicle.

Some states have laws that regulate which plants are allowed in, which aren't, and which must be quarantined. If you're moving from an area that is currently under quarantine for insects such as imported fire ants or harmful nematodes, your plants may need to be placed in a valid quarantine holding area.

Some plants may require a certificate issued by the origin state that attests that the plants are insect-free and meet quarantine requirements. It's always best to check with the agriculture department of the state you are moving to for the latest restrictions for indoor houseplants. We've included a list of the states' agriculture departments in the Resources section on page 214.

Consider the season when moving houseplants. If it's too cold or too hot, the plant can suffer and, in some cases, freeze or die from the heat. Think of them like pets. The best time to move is when temperatures are not too hot or cold. Never put plants in the trunk of a car. Avoid exposing them to direct sunlight. If you get a room for the night, you may want to bring them inside with you. If you must leave them in the vehicle, crack the windows so they have air circulation. And if it's a long drive, don't forget to give your plants a good, long drink two days before the scheduled move.

Boxes are essential when moving plants. You can group small pots together in one box. Lift hanging foliage before you add more plants to the box so that nothing is pinched between pots. Fill any extra space with crumpled paper or bubble wrap and make certain the box isn't too heavy to lift. Keep the top of the box open so that air can circulate around the plants.

Repot larger plants in lightweight, shatterproof containers and remove all dead material. Place sphagnum moss on top of the soil around the plant's base. Wrap the pot, covering the moss with plastic wrap, and secure it with tape. This will help keep the soil in the pot.

Make a sleeve with craft paper to secure the leaves and branches. Start at the base of the pot. Wrap the craft paper around the pot and secure it with tape. As you tape the sides together, gently lift the leaves and branches into the cone you're creating. The paper should create a funnel shape that supports the plant and positions the leaves upward. Don't tape the top of the paper closed.

Larger pots should each have their own, taller box; a wardrobe box works well for tall plants. Cut holes in the box for air circulation, fill empty areas around the pot with bubble wrap for cushioning and support, and don't close the top of the box.

If you can't take all your plants with you or are concerned that they won't survive the move, take cuttings of your favorites and start a new plant family when you arrive at your new home. Give the parent plants to friends or family or have a plant sale before you leave.

If you're moving plants in your car, place them on the floor of the back seat. Taller plants may need to be angled into the car or even laid on their sides. If you have rented a truck, place all plants upright and don't put anything on top of them. They should be at the rear of the truck so they're among the first to be unloaded.

Houseplants can get stressed with all the moving and atmospheric changes, but proper care before, during, and after the move can bring them back to their normal, healthy selves.

Firearms

According to 18 U.S.C. 922(a)(4) and 922(e)[10] and 27 CFR 478.28 and 478.31,[11] you may transport or ship firearms interstate when changing your state of residence, providing you lawfully possess the firearm. However, before you pack them, check the laws, both of the state and of the locality, to ensure that moving firearms into the new state does not violate any state law or local ordinance. You need to actively take steps to comply with the Firearms Owners' Protection Act,[12] which states that you have the right to move guns from one location to another, but firearms and ammunition must be separated in locked containers and inaccessible from the front of the vehicle.

If you have hired a professional moving company, you must notify them that they will be transporting firearms. Some companies have protocols in place regarding the transportation of firearms. All of them will want the guns to be unloaded.

There are certain steps to follow when transporting firearms. If you have a large gun safe, begin by removing the firearms from the safe. Don't ship the safe with the guns inside.

Ensure that all guns are unloaded and safety mechanisms are on. You can also make use of trigger locks, break the weapons down into separate pieces as an added precaution, or make the firearm inoperable by removing the bolt, firing pin, trigger assembly, and other arming parts.

Always remove all ammunition from your firearms. You cannot legally ship any live ammunition as part of your household goods. If you have ammunition that you don't want to dispose of, carry it in your private vehicle in a locked container.

If you intend to self-transport firearms in your vehicle, make sure you do not carry your weapon on your person. Check the laws of every state you will drive through on the way to your destination, including your intended route and any backup routes.

Before you lock them away, document each firearm thoroughly. Photograph each piece and write down the make, model, and serial number.

If you have individual hard cases, you can lock those and use them for transport. If you don't have cases, carefully wrap each firearm to protect and cushion it and place it in a box.

Use a code word for identification on the outside of the box. It's better not to advertise that the box is packed with firearms.

If you are using a moving company, make certain the firearm information is written on the inventory list, including make, model, serial number, unique characteristics, and caliber or gauge. Carry a copy of this information with you throughout your trip.

Chapter 10
Ready to Load?

There are some items that you will need to protect your furnishings and your back. If you don't have a dolly, rent one. It is a back-saver! It makes moving boxes and objects into the truck or container much easier. Mattress covers and moving straps can be rented through the truck rental agency. Extra blankets to prevent scratches on wood furnishings can also be rented if you haven't enough at home.

Loading the Truck or Container for a Self-Move

Moving day has arrived. Everything is organized. Boxes are clearly labeled with their contents and the room they came from. Furniture is padded and wrapped. You've properly estimated the size of the truck or container you need based on the cubic feet of your belongings. The truck is in the driveway, and you're ready to start loading it for the journey to your new home. Think of the next steps as piecing together a puzzle or playing a giant Tetris game.

The largest and heaviest things go in first. The washer should be drained, and the dryer vent hose should be disconnected and placed inside the dryer. This is best done a day or two prior to the final loading for the move. The refrigerator, washer, and dryer should be right up against the cab of the truck and should be secured with moving straps. This prevents them from squishing your other things if you have to make a fast, hard stop while on the road. Should that happen, everything moves forward, including the unsecured heavy objects.

You can put medium-sized boxes on top of the large appliances. Stack them as high as possible. Folding chairs and other filler items can be put in any extra space. The goal is to load everything as tightly as you can from the front of the cargo section of the truck to the back.

Place a mattress vertically against the big appliances and strap it in. Plastic mattress covers are very inexpensive, can be purchased at any hardware or truck rental store, and prevent your mattress from getting dirty. They are well worth the small cost.

Boxed items go in next. The heaviest boxes go on the bottom. Line them up horizontally, from side to side, right next to the mattress in the truck. Begin stacking. If the boxes are uniform, they should fit together nicely. Make each horizontal layer of boxes a little lighter in weight. Boxes marked "Fragile" go on the very top. Loading the boxes this way prevents crushing delicate items.

It's best not to use straps to secure boxes, because the corners might get crushed. The uniform size will help them stay in place during transit. Stack the boxes all the way to the top of the truck.

You can put televisions and monitors against the walls of the truck or between boxes, but always place them vertically and cushion them!

So far, the puzzle has been easy.

Once the boxes are loaded and secure, place any remaining covered mattresses vertically against the interior walls of the still-open part of truck. Secure them so they don't fall over. This will help protect and cushion the furniture, which gets loaded next.

Couches, loveseats, desks, and coffee tables can be loaded horizontally or on their sides, vertically. Provide extra padding around them and strap them in well.

You can place rolled rugs upright in the truck or on top of the boxes or furnishings. They are great for filling corners or between your pieces of furniture.

If it's a short move across town, plants can go in the back of the truck. They'll need to be supported so they don't tip over, and they need to come out first so that they don't suffer more shock than necessary. Add any odd-shaped or loose items to the cargo bay and put your two "Open first" boxes (with dining and hygiene essentials) in last.

When everything is on board, secure the door with a quality padlock and take a breath. You're almost ready to leave!

Expect that the loading process will take some time if it's a self-move. Don't push yourself too hard. You have a drive to make too. Take a break every now and then, stay hydrated, and don't forget to eat well. A piece of fruit, a quick salad, or a sandwich will provide sustainable energy where a candy bar will end in a sugar crash.

Enlist the members of your family to help and focus on their natural abilities. If one is a speedy packer and geared to getting the job done, let them. If one is better at running errands, going for food, and taking care of small details, cheer them on. Everyone can help in their own way, and that will help ease tensions.

If you're using a professional moving company, oversee what is loaded and how the furniture is handled. Once everything is onboard, the driver will give you an inventory sheet. Keep that with this book so that you'll have it when they unload at your destination.

Before You Head Out

If you are driving, make certain your vehicle is in top working order. Check the tires, oil, and filters before hitting the road. Stash an empty envelope in the glove box so that you can keep all receipts from the journey together in one place. Some of your expenses might be tax-deductible.

Saying Goodbye

If you have items such as appliance manuals to leave behind, collect them and put them in a prominent place where the new renters or owners will find them. Consider leaving written instructions on how to operate things like a security system, cameras and digital recorders, reverse osmosis water systems, or outdoor sprinkler systems.

If you have extra filters for air conditioners, heaters, or refrigerators, leave them for the new occupants. Small kindnesses like this are always appreciated.

Consider leaving a little something extra for the new occupants. Something as simple as a handwritten note wishing them the happiness you had in the residence can mean a great deal. A scented candle or gift card to a nearby restaurant is always a wonderful welcome and sure to bring a smile.

Your children might be reluctant to leave the old residence. They feel a sense of security in the familiar surroundings they've grown up in. To help them through the change, have a goodbye or appreciation ceremony for the house. Take a moment to reflect on and discuss happy events that transpired there, and then turn the focus to your next home and the possibilities that await your arrival. Memories will travel with you always, and new ones are ready to unfold.

Final Walk-Through Checklist

Before you leave the old residence, walk through to make sure you haven't forgotten something. Take pictures of each room as a form of documentation that you have left the property in good condition. This can help prevent disputes.

As you walk through, use this list to note potential issues with each room such as a stain on the carpet, a dent in the wall, or a door that doesn't latch.

Date:_____ Address: _____

_____

Outside/entry: _____

_____

Bedroom 1: _____

_____

Bedroom 2: _____

_____

Bedroom 3: _____

_____

Bedroom 4: _____

_____

Ceiling/walls: _____

_____

Carpets/flooring: _____

_____

Living room: _____

_____

Kitchen/appliances: _____

_____

Laundry: _____

_____

Dining room: _____

_____

Bathroom 1: _____

_____

Bathroom 2: _____

_____

Smoke detectors: _____

_____

Windows/screens: _____

_____

Say goodbye with appreciation for the old and welcome your new adventure.

PART 3

DURING YOUR MOVE

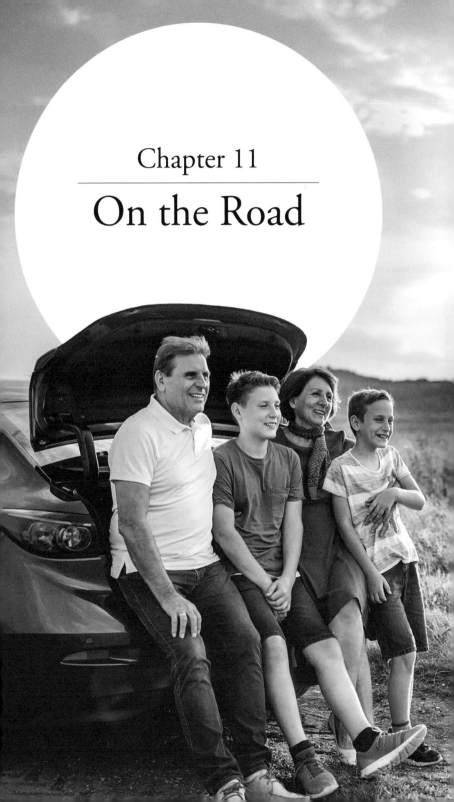

Chapter 11

On the Road

Your belongings are loaded, and now it's time to head out. You should have mapped out your route and determined where you will stop throughout the day and, when necessary, overnight. If there are multiple drivers in the household, decide who will take each leg of the journey. If you're driving, be good to yourself. Stop often to stretch, walk around, and breathe. Stay hydrated. Don't skip meals, and be sure to stop driving when you're tired. All along the way, be aware of others' needs, including children who have small bladders.

Having a company move your belongings and driving your own rental truck are different in obvious ways, but either trip can be an adventurous excursion. Driving coast-to-coast or across just one state can give you an opportunity to see things you may never see again. The US is a never-ending palette of stunning beauty. The wonder of being able to travel from boreal forests to high deserts to rolling plains to majestic mountains is an awesome experience.

Allow yourself and your family the chance to decompress from the stress that comes with a move. Even though the initial phase has been organized and smooth, it's still difficult to say goodbye to the past and hello to the future. Lingering questions may wander through your minds. Thoughts may pop up, like *Will I be happy? Will the schools be good? Will the children make friends?*

No amount of research or organization can make you happy. That's your responsibility—happiness is an inside job. If you researched the area and know the children's school is above par, don't worry. Encourage your children to be actively involved in the subjects and sports they enjoy. Give them time to grow into the new experience, and be supportive in every way you can.

No matter how much humans try, perfection is not attainable. That doesn't mean you shouldn't stop setting your version of perfect as a goal, but it does mean you should relax when something doesn't quite measure up to your standards. Just work to improve it.

Your upcoming drive is an excellent example. You can rush, try to drive straight through, skip meals or gulp down fast food, and push on even though you know you're tired and your body is rebelling, or you can add some pleasure to your journey. When something doesn't quite go as planned—and it probably won't (that's life)—try to think a few years ahead and view the situation from that perspective. A few years from now, you'll be able to laugh, or at least smirk, at the fact that you didn't get on the road at the precise time you'd planned because the shower in the motel wasn't working properly or the car overheated and you were towed backward through a town celebrating Crazy Days where everyone waved because they thought you were part of the festivities. It might be frustrating or embarrassing in the moment, but years from now, you'll remember those incidents fondly and giggle.

Make a mini vacation of the trip, and let it help you and the family unwind from the stress of everything you've already done. Plan your route according to things that might interest you. Whether you spend an afternoon at the Grand Canyon, drive a portion of Route 66, or visit the world's largest ball of twine, there is something interesting out there for everyone. History buffs traveling Interstate 40 might want to visit the Billy the Kid Museum in New Mexico, or there's the Alamo Visitor Center and Museum off Interstate 10 in Texas. Spend a relaxing afternoon at Hot Springs National Park in Arkansas off I-40 or absorb the beauty of Gulf Islands National Seashore Park, which runs from Mississippi to Florida off I-10. From mansions to museums, battleships to bayous, there are any numbers of sights that await you.

In the resources section at the back of this book, you'll find links to national parks, state parks, and unusual places to visit in the US.

Traveling with Kids

If you are using the time in the car as a family holiday, consider ways to keep the children entertained. If the kids aren't prone to car sickness, DVDs, tablets, and books are some of the best options, especially if they're using headphones. Audiobooks, verbal games, singing, and enjoying the beauty of the countryside are alternatives for those who should keep their gazes trained out the window to avoid nausea.

DEVRA'S TIPS

- Find some travel versions of popular board games, especially if you have more than one child—they can play together.
- Have snacks handy. Hungry children can get cranky, and you can never have enough snacks.
- Reading and coloring books are entertaining.
- Try a family sing-along.
- Don't mention the toilet unless you're planning to stop.
- Download several of their favorite games or movies to a tablet or other digital device, or have a portable DVD player with several titles available.
- Headphones are a must. They can enjoy their music or games, and the rest of car doesn't have to be "entertained."
- A favorite blanket, stuffed animal, or pillow is comforting.
- Stop at places where they can run around and wear off some of their abundant energy.
- Have patience and plan for the trip to take longer than it would if you were alone.

Instead of eating at a restaurant, plan lunch as a family picnic. The time outside will give the kids a chance to burn off some of their natural energy.

A child will need potty stops more frequently than the adults, and you're bound to hear, "Are we there yet?" more times than you can count, but the memories formed on the trip are worth the experience.

Traveling with Pets

Traveling with pets can also be an exercise in patience, especially if the animals are not accustomed to being in a vehicle. Secure them in a carrier or with a seat safety harness and make sure they have access to water. They'll need their own potty stops and some exercise after being in one spot for a few hours. Many will require a calmative, either prescribed by the veterinarian or an over-the-counter version.

Devra's daughter, Rebecca, recalls her unruly singing cat that wasn't fond of radios:

> My mom and I were moving back to Arizona from North Carolina to care for my grandparents. We were each driving our cars, and the movers were already on their merry way with our furniture. Mom had suggested that I talk to the vet about getting my cat a tranquilizer for the trip, but I'd traveled with animals before and never had a problem. I didn't think it was necessary.
>
> I turned on the radio, and the cat started screaming. It was a horrible screeching sound, so loud that my ears ached. I'd turn off the radio, and it would stop. I'd turn it on, and it would start up again. I turned off the radio and hoped it was a passing thing.
>
> We'd planned to make it to Atlanta the first night, but I barely made it to the Georgia border. I motioned Mom to pull over. As she was getting out of her car, I was pulling the cat carrier out of my car.

I set it on the curb and asked the cat if it wanted to live in Georgia. Mom nearly doubled over from laughter.

DEVRA'S TIPS

- Get medication for pets that are traveling with you by plane or car. Use it when—and if—necessary.
- Don't feed your pet in the car or right before you start out on your journey. Some animals get carsick. They will enjoy the meal when you stop at the end of the day.
- If they are in a crate or carrier, make sure it's big enough for them to stand and move around while they're constrained.
- Keep their area well ventilated. Pets can overheat easily, especially if they are not accustomed to a car.
- If possible, keep your cat where they can see you. This seems to calm them.
- Play with your cat before you leave.
- Consider using pheromones to help calm your pets.
- Puppies and senior dogs may need more frequent bathroom breaks.
- Senior dogs need to stretch more often.
- Make sure your pet is microchipped, and always keep them on a secure leash when they are out of their carrier.
- Make them feel comfortable with one of your T-shirts to curl up on in their crate so they feel your presence.
- Thunder shirts and anti-anxiety medicine can help calm them.
- Never, ever leave them unattended in a vehicle.

I handed the carrier to Mom. Mom loaded the cat in her car, and for the rest of the trip, I played my radio. Mom traveled in silence cross-country. Neither one of us thought of purchasing a calmative. That was a big lesson we learned.[13]

Overnight Stops

Map out your trip, noting the areas you intend to stay in overnight. If you have pets with you, before you start the trip, locate the hotels or motels that will let them stay with you. It's best to have a room reserved so that you know you have a place to rest. Find out what the cancelation policy is if you don't make it to your destination due to unforeseen circumstances.

As you travel, always lock all vehicles and make certain that they are secure and parked in a well-lit area.

Some people like to drive as far as they can each day before they drop from sheer exhaustion or their buns and calves cramp. They hope they will find an establishment in that spot that's flashing a big vacancy sign. That's not always the case.

A close friend, Brett Nilsson, told us about an uncomfortable experience he and his fiancée had while moving to Washington state for his new job. They had a time constraint and planned to push themselves to the limit every day. He recalls:

We got an early-morning start on the first day of what I expected to be a three-day interstate trip. I was driving a rental truck and towing my Civic. We wanted to get as far as we could each day, so we didn't make arrangements for specific hotels along our planned route. The first day was a breeze. We found a clean little hotel and crashed for the night so we could start out early again the next day.

The second day I pushed myself a little more. It was about sunset, and I decided we could easily make it to the next town. Surely there were more hotel choices. The sun had been down for a couple of hours when we rolled in. It was true, there were more hotels, but every last one of them had "NO Vacancy" signs blazing. I'd waited too late in the night to stop.

We found an empty section of a parking lot outside one of the larger chain hotels, locked up the truck, and climbed into the little Civic to try to get some sleep. We put sunscreens in the windows for some semblance of privacy and tried to get comfortable. I loved my Civic, but it wasn't designed for sleeping, especially when you're six-foot-one.[14]

DEVRA'S TIP There are so many similar stories of people who wanted to drive as far as they could each day and chose not to make reservations. Driving is tiring, and you need proper rest. Know when to stop. Pick an area where you have scoped out the hotels/motels and make a reservation.

Weather

Check what the weather will be along your route before you start driving. Knowing what to anticipate can help you plan your trip more safely. If the northern or high-elevation route is snow covered and icy, you might need to take a southern or lower-elevation route. Estimate the extra time it will take to complete the journey and plan accordingly.

Know what weather will greet you when you arrive so you can be prepared. If you're leaving three feet of snow and arriving in eighty-degree sunshine, make certain you're prepared with lightweight, light-colored clothing. If you are going into serious weather, it might be wise to hold your trip for a day or two if you can.

Devra lived a nightmare by not checking what the weather would be when she arrived from dry air and sunshine to the East Coast:

> We left on a clear, sunny day, drove three days, and arrived in our rental truck during a Category 3 hurricane. Fighting wind gusts of eighty miles per hour and the hardest rain I'd ever seen, we unloaded our rental truck in a completely disorganized, throw-and-go way. It was dark, and no one had power. Hotels were either full or evacuated. We had no choice but to tough it out until the power was restored and we could set about reorganizing our lives.

DEVRA'S TIP Proper planning can prevent poor performance. Checking the extended forecast can alert you to possible weather-related issues.

Have a Contact Person

One of the most important tips for any length of drive is to let others know what route you are taking. Designate a daily contact person you can check in with while you're on the road. This provides a sense of security for you and your family and friends. In your daily call or text, give them an updated schedule, if there have been any changes, and let them know your estimated destination for the next day.

Texts or calls are a lifeline in case there is an emergency. Knowing that someone expects to hear from you every day is comforting to everyone involved.

Don't take detours from your original route without letting someone know that you've made a change of plans. Sometimes it is necessary because of road construction or other issues, but always, *always* inform your designated contact before you embark on a different path.

DEVRA'S TIP Share your planned route with your contact person and stick to the plan. A major interstate provides services every so often, so when possible, stay on the main freeway.

Devra was once stranded in Texas because she took an alternate route.

There was an announcement of bad weather ahead, so we made a last-minute decision to take an alternate route, which was a two-lane highway. From that we could eventually jump north to Interstate 40. I'd never taken this road and couldn't find much information about it on the map. We were flying blind, as they say.

The road was not marked well, and the pavement was patchy. For miles, we saw nothing, and no one passed us going the other way. It became very clear very fast that we were out in the middle of nowhere, Texas.

Suddenly the car bounced as I hit something in the road that I had not seen because of a major dip. I didn't dare stop. For miles and miles, I watched the tire pressure slowly decline. There was no place to stop and get the help I needed. The car was starting to pull to the left, but thankfully, I could see the interstate ahead.

I pulled off the road. I found a deer antler sticking out of the side of my tire. The car was fully packed, and it would have been quite a task to empty the whole thing out in order to get to the tiny spare tire in the back.

On an almost-flat tire, we limped into a semitruck repair shop at the first exit just inside the New Mexico border. Because they had no way to repair a tire of this size, they sent a man back to a town in Texas to get a replacement tire. We sat for four hours in the heat with our dogs waiting for him to return. They changed out the tire, but because they didn't usually work on cars, they couldn't reset all the sensors, so I drove the next two days with the low-tire light flashing on my dash.

Manage Your Essentials

You've planned well for traveling with your children and pets, but what about you? A long drive can be taxing, even when you plan to make it as enjoyable as possible. The four primary things to keep in mind are that you will need rest, nourishing food, fluids, and patience. Metaphorical bumps in the road occur no matter how well you have planned. Be flexible. Try not to overreact when the unexpected pops up—recognize that some things are beyond your control. Literally take a deep breath and clear your mind of emotional reaction as you exhale. That simple step can help you focus on the problem at hand without the encumbrance of an emotional reaction.

Rather than eating heavy meals as you travel, opt for lighter fare that you can bring with you. Portable food heaters, ovens, and coolers are all available for purchase, and all you need is a 12V converter. Most vehicles have a 12V converter, or a cigarette lighter, somewhere on the dash or console. Just plug in the pot and begin heating your meal. Plug-in 12V coolers are great for keeping water chilled and salads or sandwiches fresh. And they are a must-have if you have medications that require refrigeration.

Soups, salads, and lean protein will carry your physical energy and mental clarity further than heavy carbohydrates and processed sugars. Carbs and sugars tend to give a burst of energy followed by a reduction of physical and mental functions.

Keep healthy snacks handy. Nuts, edamame, popcorn, trail mix, and fruits are good to graze on between meals. They are simple, filling, healthy, and help maintain your get-up-and-go.

Staying hydrated is an absolute must. Sodas and coffee don't replace water. To make certain that you are staying hydrated, add in some electrolytes, which will help your body balance fluids within and outside of your cells. They help regulate a variety of your body's most essential functions, including nerve signaling, pH balance, and muscle contraction.

Rest is essential. If your drive requires more than seven hours in your vehicle, it's best to plan an overnight stay somewhere. Without the proper sleep, your response time is slowed, and this puts your and your family's safety, as well as that of other drivers, at risk.

DEVRA'S TIPS

- Allow ample travel time.
- Plan your route and share that information with your designated contact.
- Dress comfortably. Avoid tight-fitting clothing.
- Take a break every two or three hours.
- Stretch and practice breathing techniques during your break.
- If possible, share the responsibility of driving with someone else.
- Don't rely solely on cruise control. A lack of driver involvement can lead to a lack of concentration.
- Avoid distractions like cell phones. Pull over and take a call if you must.
- Be courteous to other drivers. (Wave with your whole hand, not just one finger.)

You're almost to your new home!

PART 4

AFTER YOUR MOVE

Chapter 12

Arriving at Your New Home

You've arrived at your new residence, and it feels like there's still so much to be done. The final stages of getting settled will be easier if you've followed the guidelines on the previous pages.

Just as planning before packing will allow things to go more smoothly, it's important to take a moment to plan prior to unloading and unpacking. Before anything enters the house or apartment, take a walk-through of the place and photograph every room, including closets. Pay attention to any damage. Look for water stains on the ceiling, which could indicate a leaky pipe. Do the windows have screens on them? Do doors and windows close tightly? Are the carpets stained? Do they need to be cleaned? Are there any odd odors? Are there any signs of insects? How clean are the rooms? Is the electricity, gas, and water turned on? If you have natural gas or propane appliances already in the residence, are the pilot lights properly working?

Walk-through Checklist

Use this checklist to make note of any issues you find during the walkthrough.

Date:_____ Address: _____

_____

Outside/entry: _____

_____

Bedroom 1: _____

_____

Bedroom 2: _____

_____

Bedroom 3: _____

_____

Bedroom 4: _____

_____

Ceiling/walls: _____

_____

Carpets/flooring: _____

_____

Living room: _____

_____

Kitchen/appliances: _____

_____

Laundry: _____

_____

Dining room: _____

_____

Bathroom 1: _____

_____

Bathroom 2: _____

_____

Smoke detectors: _____

_____

Windows/screens: _____

_____

Write down and photograph all items you're uncomfortable with and bring them to the attention of the property manager or realtor. Devra experienced an issue with pests that became apparent soon after she entered the apartment. It is rare, but it can happen.

I was very young at the time, and this was one of my first moves, so I didn't really think about the fact that there might be bugs in the carpet when I moved into my new apartment.

I was so excited to be in my new home. I unlocked the door and stepped inside wearing my brand-new white jeans. As I showed my best gal pal around the apartment, gloating about where all my furniture would be placed, she suddenly looked alarmed and said, "Weren't you wearing white pants when we came in?"

I looked down, and to my horror, I was covered with little dots of bouncing brown things. They were fleas! The whole apartment was infested with fleas. I immediately went to the apartment manager's office and showed her my pants. I was told that the carpets had been cleaned from the previous tenants, but the management office was not responsible for pest control; that was up to the tenants. I didn't realize different locations had different ordinances and assumed that everyone sprayed for bugs before a new tenant moved in.

DEVRA'S TIP Always ask the landlord if the property has been sprayed for bugs. If not, ask if they will spray before you move in. If they won't accommodate that request, it's up to you to spray or use a bug bomb before you move in. If you have pets or children, make certain that the insecticide is nontoxic to them.

After you've noted any repairs that need to be made, either by a professional or the property manager, and are satisfied with the cleanliness and lack of creepy-crawlies, grab the boxes that you labeled "Open first." You'll have the essentials to get you through the first steps of moving in. If your new home has a refrigerator and you have power, put any perishable items you picked up along the way in the fridge. You'll have chilled water, juice, cold drinks, and whatever else you've brought along to sustain you.

Do You Need Help?

If you've rented a truck or container, ask the company for references of individuals who can help you unload. If they don't have any in the area, try some of the resources listed in the back of this book or get on local social media and ask who other newcomers have used. References are important because you are new to the area and want to feel secure in the people you select.

If you've hired a professional moving company, they do the heavy lifting and follow your directions as to the placement of furniture and boxes.

The Waiting Game

If you used a professional moving line, there is a strong possibility that your belongings will be arriving at your new home days after you do. You have a choice of either camping out in the residence and waiting for your furniture or taking up temporary residence at a hotel. That decision may depend on your budget, agility, age, and sense of adventure. If you are up to roughing it, air mattresses and/or sleeping bags are inexpensive ways to assure that you can at least get some rest while you wait.

Whether you're staying in a hotel or camping in your new living room, get a delivery date from the driver. In the meantime, explore your new city or town. Locate grocery stores, where you'll be going to work every day, playgrounds, dog parks, and the children's school(s). Both children and adults will feel more comfortable when the first day of class begins if you know where you are going. Scoping out the local markets will give you an idea of local produce and let you stock the refrigerator with nutritious, comforting snacks. If you have access to a washer and dryer, this waiting period is an ideal time to catch up on laundry from the move.

This is also a good time to child- or pet-proof your new residence, change the locks on the doors, change the batteries in fire and carbon monoxide detectors, check for fire extinguishers, and purchase new ones when needed. If your new home has a security system, familiarize yourself and the family with all aspects of it. This downtime is also a good moment to check on schedules and regulations pertaining to garbage and recycling pickup in your neighborhood.

Time is never wasted unless you let it be wasted. If you stay active and busy, time seems to move much faster.

Furniture First

Whether you have self-moved or hired a professional moving company, unloading the furniture first is important because you don't want to be tripping over boxes as you try to position heavier objects like couches and desks. If some boxes do come off the truck or out of the container before the furniture, place them away from traffic areas. If a box goes in a bedroom and the bed and dresser haven't come off the truck, stash the box in the closet.

Determine Where You Want Your Furniture

No matter whether you made the trek to your new residence in a rental truck or your belongings are arriving via container or van, take your time unloading. As the furniture comes off the truck or out of the container, place it in the room where it belongs and position it where you want it.

It is best to have a basic layout in mind before everything gets moved into the house. You are the director of this episode. If you've hired people to help you unload, you might want to put Post-it notes on the walls where the furniture goes. This will make it easier for you and for them. There may be three people unloading, all wanting directions at the same time. If you've posted notes on the doors that identify "Billy's room" or "Primary bedroom" and notes inside the rooms marking the locations for "Billy's room, bed" or "Primary bedroom, dresser," it's easier for you to point to the room and tell them to follow the directions on the notes.

Put together the bed frames and arrange them where you want them in each bedroom. When the mattresses come in, they will have frames waiting for them. By putting the frames together first, when the boxes come into the room, you won't have to move them another time to put the bed together. Don't let the unloading process fall into chaos by having to move boxes from here to there and back again.

If you have children, let them help put lighter boxes in their rooms. Let them know that when everything has been unloaded, it will be up to them to unpack the boxes and put their things where they want them. Reassure the younger ones that you'll be there if they need help, and let the older ones have freer rein in decisions about their space. Letting them make determinations about their rooms promotes a sense of empowerment. This is all new to them too, and it might create a little angst for them. You have the life experiences to adapt to change more easily, while they need subtle forms of support.

As the Boxes Come off the Truck

If possible, completely unload the truck or container before you call it a day. You don't want any of your belongings left in a vehicle parked on the street. Otherwise, be sure to lock it securely with a padlock.

As the day wears on, you will be happy that the boxes are all marked with the room they should be placed in. You will find it makes the unloading operation smooth for everyone involved.

Unpacking

Unpack the boxes that hold items you will need first. Sheets for the beds, fresh pajamas, towels, washcloths, hygiene products, and anything else that you absolutely need are the best starting points. You'll probably need some essentials unpacked for the kitchen if you didn't have enough kitchen items packed in the "Open first" boxes. Have the children unpack their clothing and less-fun belongings before their toys and books. Chances are they won't finish unpacking the rest of their boxes once the entertainment comes out.

Next, find the boxes that hold your televisions and computers. Any cable, satellite, internet, and/or telephone installers you scheduled before you left the old residence should be arriving in the next day or two. You'll need the electronic devices unpacked, positioned, and ready so that the installers can test internet and cable connections when they arrive. (Hopefully they will arrive per the schedule you arranged prior to the move.)

Don't attempt to unpack and arrange everything as soon as you've unloaded. It's a process. It may be a bit frustrating having boxes everywhere, but it's vital that you rest, eat, hydrate, and think things through. Take the time to figure out exactly where you want the dishes and pots and pans to go; what goes in a cabinet and what goes on the counter. Then try to relax and unwind a little before you sleep. Tomorrow is another day.

Preparing the Rental Truck Return

If you've rented a truck, clean it out well. That includes sweeping it down so you aren't charged a cleaning fee. Blankets, dollies, straps, and anything else that you may have rented from the company should be free of damage and stored neatly in the back of the truck.

Check the cab and make certain nothing is left in the glove box or other compartments. If you spilled anything in the cab, clean the area before you return the truck.

On your way to the truck rental company, be certain to stop and fill the tank with gas. It's just like a rental car: if you return it empty or even half-full, you will be charged the rental company's rate for the missing fuel, which is usually quite high.

Finishing a Container Move

Once everything is unloaded from the container, sweep it out and call the company to arrange a pickup. The container has served its purpose.

Follow Through

All the information you recorded in chapter 4, "Services to Schedule for Connection," will come in handy now. Your electricity and gas should be turned on and your internet, cable, and telephone installed. It's also time to take care of the little details that can easily be overlooked, like calling your insurance company to make necessary updates to your policies or organizing what you'll need to get the children registered in their new schools.

Contact the Schools

If you have children, contact the school(s) they will be attending and schedule an appointment to get them registered. If you know the school before the move, it's wise to save time and make the call before you relocate. If you don't have that information before the move, try to contact the schools right after you arrive at your new home. Ask the school what documents they need. Find out if your child can register online or if they must appear at the school with proper documentation.

Does the school need medical records, education records, and transcripts? Can the children's records be submitted digitally? Some states require a copy of the custody agreement if the parents are divorced, so ask about that. If there are any legal actions against the noncustodial parent, provide that paperwork, as well. Ask if students are required to wear a uniform, and if so, where they might be purchased. You don't want a last-minute document search or shopping trip to get the kids ready for their first day at a new school.

Credit Card Companies, Your Bank, and Bills

Let your bank and credit card companies know that you are no longer traveling. Verify that they have your new address on file.

If your old bank does not have offices in your new location, shop around for banks or credit unions that offer the services you need. If your bank does have a branch nearby, then you'll want to update your mailing and billing address. Set up new accounts when necessary, and consider setting up automatic withdrawals for your monthly bills.

Get online and update your new address for any monthly subscriptions or billings. Amazon, PayPal, and other companies will require this. Magazine subscriptions, whether online or hard copy, will also need to be updated with your new address.

Contact Your Insurance Companies

Contact your homeowner's or renter's insurance company. If you moved within the same state, provide your new address and ask if they need to transfer your policy to a new agent or office.

If you have moved out of state, let them know your new location and see if there will be any changes to your policy. Some companies do not have coverage from one state to another. If your renter's insurance or house insurance does not transfer to the new residence, immediately find a company whose policy meets your needs. If you are renting, ask your property manager about good companies with decent rates or reach out to a real estate rental agent for suggestions.

Many medical and dental insurance plans do not transfer from state to state. Contact your old insurer and find out if your coverage will be active in your new location. If not, and the company has offices in your new area, reach out to an agent and design a policy. If the company does not work in your new area, reach out to an insurance broker to help you find the right company and policies to fill your needs. If you have to switch companies, cancel your old medical insurance in writing.

Notify Medicare and Social Security of your new address too.

Vehicle insurance usually transfers from state to state. Contact your old agent and let them know you have arrived at your new home. The agent will probably hand you off to a new office. There may be alterations to your policy, which might include lower or higher payments. Ask questions about coverage in your new state and design the policy for your current needs. In many cases, vehicle insurance can be taken care of on the phone.

Contact Your Post Office and the Pharmacy of Your Choice

If your mail has been forwarded to your new address, pick it up and let the post office know you have moved in and regular delivery can begin. You should also get your prescriptions transferred or drop off any new scripts that your doctor provided before the move. This way they will be ready when you need them. These are two important items that should be seen to right away.

Quick Checklist

Here's an at-a-glance overview of things you will want to address soon after your move. Use the list to check off tasks as you complete them.

___ School(s) contacted
___ School paperwork gathered
___ School supplies purchased
___ Credit card companies—new billing address verified
___ Banks—new address verified
___ New bank—accounts opened
___ New monthly bills set up
___ Existing monthly bills—new address verified
___ Renter's insurance—updated or changed
___ Homeowner's insurance—updated or changed
___ Medicare and social security—new address updated
___ Medical insurance—updated or changed
___ Dental insurance—updated or changed
___ Vision insurance—updated or changed
___ Vehicle insurance—updated or changed
___ Vehicle registration—updated or changed
___ Driver's license—updated or changed
___ Voter registration—updated or changed
___ Pharmacy contacted

During the Next Thirty Days

Medical Professionals

Review the medical professionals in your area; determine what type of specialists you need and what you are looking for in a general practitioner (GP). Once your medical insurance takes effect, make any appointments that you feel are necessary. The first appointment should be to establish a doctor-patient relationship with a general practitioner. Do this as soon as possible. Having a general practitioner helps you avoid trips to urgent care. A GP can recommend specialists you may need to see and get your prescriptions set up at the local pharmacy.

Sometimes it can be difficult to get in to see a GP, as Devra learned on her last move to Northern California:

> When I arrived, I discovered there was a shortage of doctors in town. There was a six-month wait to be seen for the first time, and that was true for every member of my family.
>
> It created havoc with the prescriptions that had to be refilled on a continual basis and meant we had to use urgent care facilities, which were not covered by our medical insurance. Fortunately, my previous cardiologist had put through a referral to another cardiologist in the area, so there was no waiting for the treatment of an ongoing heart condition.

DEVRA'S TIP If possible, have your doctor(s) give you referrals to doctors in the new city. Send copies of your records to any physician or specialist you may need in your new location.

Remember, when you are meeting a physician for the first time, you are interviewing them for the position of caring for your health. Tell them exactly what you need and see if there is solid communication between the two of you. There is no requirement that you settle for the first doctor you meet. You might have to go through two or three such interviews before you find a fit that works medically and feels comfortable to you.

Vehicles and Licenses

If you have made an interstate move, you will need to get a new driver's license and re-register your vehicle(s) in your new state. In most states, you have thirty days to get to the Department of Motor Vehicles

(DMV) to change your vehicle registration and get a new driver's license. Getting a new license might require taking a test. If that is the case, study the regulations online or stop by the closest DMV office and pick up a booklet that details state laws. Each state has different laws, although the basics like "Which road sign is a red octagon?" will remain the same throughout the country.

If you are in the military or you're a college student, you might not need to change your driver's license or vehicle registration. Check the laws of the state you are stationed in or attending college in.

If you own other vehicles such as all-terrain vehicles (ATVs), recreational vehicles, a motor home, motorcycles, snowmobiles, or a tractor, check the local laws and register them as well. Trailers must be registered if they are going to be on the road. It doesn't matter if they are travel or camp trailers, fifth wheels, horse trailers, or hauling trailers, they have to be tagged and registered in the new state.

Registering a boat varies from state to state. Research the boat registration requirements in your state. At some point you will need to complete a registration form, which is commonly found online, but you may need to apply in person. You will need to provide proof of ownership via a title and/or bill of sale and then pay the registration fee, which will vary by state and according to the size of the boat.

A jet ski is considered a Class A inboard watercraft by the US Coast Guard and follows the rules for other boats. Jet skis must be registered if they are operated on a public waterway. In some states you not only need proper documentation but an operator's license as well. Research the rules in your area to prevent unnecessary frustration on your outings.

Cleaning Out the Clutter

If you changed locations as a job requirement, gather all your receipts from the move, as you may be able to use them as a tax deduction. Keep everything, including food, hotel, vehicle rental, and fuel receipts, in an envelope and put it in the file for this year's taxes.

Once you have everything unpacked and put in its proper place, it's time to get rid of the boxes and packing materials. Break down the boxes so that they lay flat and take up less space. Contact the truck rental company to see if they will take used boxes—sometimes they will if you were a customer. If you choose to recycle them, make sure they are broken down completely and remove any tape that may still be attached to the cardboard. One of the fastest ways to make all the packing clutter vanish is to post on local social media pages that you have free boxes and materials available to be picked up. They're usually gone in a day!

PART 5

OTHER TYPES OF MOVES

Chapter 13
Military Moves

M ilitary moves can provide a means of seeing the world. If you are active-duty military, you are probably going to move multiple times over the course of your career. It may be cross-country, across the state, or internationally, but chances are you will experience a permanent change of station, known as a PCS. A PCS can happen abruptly or with ample time to plan, but there are basically two options available to you: 1) the military makes all arrangements for you and carries out the move, or 2) you do it yourself.

It's impossible to cover the intricacies of a military move in this book, but here are some basics to get your started.

Whichever type of move you select, begin by contacting your local transportation office. They can walk you through things like entitlements, which are the amount and type of items you are allowed to move and your moving allowance.

According to the Military OneSource website,

> Moving allowance generally refers to the overall weight of your household goods. The rank specified on your job/travel orders will be used to determine your total weight allowance. In general, as your rank increases, your moving allowance also increases. Any cost to move additional items/weight above your moving allowance will be charged to you after delivery, so work hard to make sure you stay within your weight allowance.[15]

The weight allowances vary not only based on rank but also based on number of dependents and the type of move. There is a difference in allotments for a PCS move and a temporary duty (TDY) move. Allowances also might differ between branches of the service, which makes it important for you to work through your local transportation office to thoroughly understand your individual entitlements.

When moving, you can choose for the military to provide a company to do all the hard work. They bring in a transportation service provider, called a TSP, who packs everything, loads it all, and arranges for storage until it is shipped to your new location. Heads-up—your furnishings sometimes take a while to arrive. Everything is insured for loss and damage, but you might have to wait a while for it. You are working on their schedule, not yours. A TSP is often the best alternative for single military households that have received last-minute orders or when your family is being stationed overseas.

The more common option is called a personally procured move (PPM), also known as a do-it-yourself move (DITY). A PPM is basically a self-move. You pack, you load, you arrange the transportation, and finally, you unload, unpack, and arrange for the return of the transportation to its source. Many personnel prefer the PPM, as the government reimburses your out-of-pocket expenses based on the rate it would pay for a TSP move. PPMs are great for continental US moves (or CONUS). CONUS covers the contiguous states and Washington, DC.

There is a possible combination of a TSP and a PPM. It's called a partial-PPM. This allows the government to contract movers for part of the shipment—usually the heavy furnishings—while you take care of boxing and transporting the smaller items. A PPM that's referred to as "you load/they drive" is also popular choice for service members.

If you are being stationed overseas, are put on temporary assignment, or receive OCONUS orders, a container company might be a good option for you. OCONUS refers to domestic moves outside the continental US, including Alaska, Hawaii, and the US territories of Guam, Puerto Rico, American Samoa, and US Saipan. OCONUS does not include foreign countries.

1-800-PACK-RAT has been very helpful to many military families who select a PPM. We asked James L. Burati III, the Chief Sales Officer, why that is:

> At 1-800-PACK-RAT, we have a lot of employees, family, and friends who have served in the military, and we have the utmost respect and appreciation of their sacrifices. We want to ensure that all veterans and active-duty members, as well as their families, can trust us to move and store their belongings at the lowest prices we are able to offer. We also know that our moving and storage solutions can make PCSing a lot less stressful for families since we deliver a container, pick the packed container up, and move and re-deliver all on their schedule. And we know things can change quickly with military moves, so our flexible storage options can really help when customers get to their new location and may need some extra time to find their new home. We also have trusted third-party service providers who can help pack and load your belongings as well as pick up and deliver your vehicles to your new home. No need to stress over packing and unloading on your own or having to put unnecessary wear and tear on your vehicle or go through the process of selling it to avoid the hassle.[16]

Burati added that 1-800-PACK-RAT offers military families "flexibility and peace of mind knowing their stuff is safe and can be re-routed if needed or stored at a warehouse as needed." He continued:

> It is a much better solution than the typical van lines where your belongings are loaded with other goods and you have no tracking or visibility into where your stuff is or when it will arrive. You also have no flexibility—once it is on the truck, it is going to the location you provided, and you cannot make

any changes. That is not how we do it—you have your own container, and if you need to make any changes, just call us.[17]

Some of the options provided to service members include the ability to move military service members across the continental United States and assist in local moves. He explained:

> We know that even local moves can be tricky, so we make it easier by bringing the container directly to the customer's home, they have as much time to pack as needed, then we can bring their container directly to their new home or keep it in storage for as long as needed. This provides a lot more flexibility and convenience, especially compared to rental trucks that you need to get everything done in one day![18]

They also offer on-site storage, with over sixty-five secure warehouse storage facilities across the US. This puts them in a perfect position to provide warehouse storage wherever service members are stationed, whether it's in the US or on foreign soil.

If you need help with packing, loading, car shipping, or moving supplies, 1-800-PACK-RAT can help. And best of all, they offer a discount for military members.

The military does reimburse many of your PCS moving expenses, which might include packing supplies, rental trucks or portable containers, and fuel. If you follow the cost-saving, easy steps throughout this book, you'll probably be able to save money and maybe pocket some extra cash, as well as have a happy, organized, and less stressful experience.

Assistance Programs

Military relocation assistance programs are available to you to help navigate housing and childcare options, both on and off base, area schools, spousal employment, and license transfers. Programs that are available to you largely depend on the location of your duty orders.

Moving Your Family

You and your family will be provided transportation and a per diem allowance to help cover food and lodging expenses along the way to your new station. The amount is determined based on the number of travel days that have been authorized for the move.

The location of your new duty station may prevent the shipment of all your belongings or your personal vehicle. If that is the case, see if you can obtain a storage authorization for the items left behind.

You may also be provided a dislocation allowance (DLA) that is designed to help partially reimburse expenses that are not normally covered in a move, like utility deposits. These are generally allotted once per year.

Temporary lodging expenses may be provided to you and your dependents. This usually covers the first ten days after you've reached your new assignment station.

Children

Children of military personnel have to change residences, schools, and even countries far more often than most children. This can be disconcerting and make them feel a little insecure, as they don't have time to create lasting bonds of friendship and are constantly being introduced to new aspects of life.

Family support is key for them to develop into strong, independent individuals. Dr. Donna Marks, who wrote the foreword to this book, was raised in a military family, and although it was traumatic at the time, she appreciates all the experiences that made her the resilient, self-sufficient woman she is today.

I was raised in the Air Force, and we kids are often referred to as Air Force brats. I have no idea how the term got started, but being branded as brats is the farthest thing from the truth. Relocation to the next base on short notice requires the flexibility to upend our lives at a moment's notice. The upheaval of packing and unpacking, friending and unfriending, adjusting and readjusting can be overwhelming. Unfortunately, tender roots are never allowed to take hold and anchor to anything solid before it's time to move on.

While I felt like moving all the time was a curse and indeed uncomfortable during childhood, it turned out to be a blessing in the long run. I learned to be flexible and adapt to just about any situation. I'm always up for an impromptu trip and can have my bag packed and be ready to go at a moment's notice. Even though my early education was poor due to so many interruptions, psychological challenges, and subpar classrooms, it didn't deter my desire to learn. I always have a book at hand and an ever-burning passion for grabbing as much knowledge as possible in this life of abundant opportunities. I never attended a boarding school or an Ivy League college, but the military life provided educational experiences that don't come from traditional education. A strong sense of adventure has led me the world over, to common and uncommon experiences. Having mastered the art of moving, I converted that skill into a hobby to remodel homes and then sell at a profit. Juggling several careers at once is natural for someone who frequently relocated during childhood. My time alone and solitude have given me an ongoing appreciation of the soothing elements of nature, and it's always been a source of spiritual connection that I found in those early strolls through the woodlands of Labrador. I learned to put my roots into things that last, like sunsets and waterfalls, the elements, swooshing waves, giant blueberries, midnight skies, and crackling twigs underfoot. These things held me then and will always be there to console me through life's twists and turns that forever move us around.[19]

Pets

In some cases, your pets are permitted to make the PSC move with you. The limit is usually two pets per family, and there is a weight limit. Your local transportation office will make the connection to Patriot Express pet services, which provide transportation for your furry family members.

You are responsible for the fees, health documentation, and kennels for transportation. Pet spaces are limited on Patriot Express and are generally booked 90 to 120 days in advance of the move. They are done on a first-come, first-served basis, so it is important to contact your local transportation office as soon as you receive your assignment.

Travel from state to state or from country to country will require that your pet meet certain specific health requirements. The Animal and Plant Health Inspection Service (APHIS) makes those determinations. The website for APHIS can be found in the resources at the back of this book.

If you are unable to take your pet with you when you move, there are places to board your pet with a loving family. Please see the resources section for more information.

Travel Restrictions

Based on your new location, you or members of your family may be restricted from traveling to certain areas or patronizing certain businesses. You should check with your supervisor or contact your local transportation office once you receive orders.

Research and Get Assistance for Your Needs

Military OneSource, a Department of Defense–funded program, is one of your greatest resources for your military move and eventual relocation. Not only is this resource designed to help with the initial phases of moving but they can also help determine what assets are available at your new station. You can find links to their website in the resources section at the back of the book.

Chapter 14
International Moves

The US Department of State estimates that nine million American citizens were living abroad between 2019 and 2020.[20] If you are preparing to join those millions of individuals by making an international move, you should begin researching months in advance. It takes a lot of planning and attention to detail. Things will be different. Food, language, housing, and customs will not be what you're accustomed to, and learning about the country, its people, its language, and its culture will benefit you tremendously.

Every country has its own set of rules and regulations for immigrants. Whether you're moving for work, to study, or because you want a lifestyle change, visit the website of the country's consulate to gain a better understanding of what is required of you. To begin with, if your journey is more than a vacation of a limited time span, you will probably need a visa.

Visas

As soon as you know that you will be moving outside the country, secure proper visas for yourself and your family. You'll need passports, birth certificates, divorce decrees, child custody documents, proof of employment or financial stability, and possibly more based on the country's requirements.

Applying for a visa needs to be done long before you move. There are different types of visas, and you'll have to determine which is appropriate for you. The most common are work visas and student visas, but there are others, and the type will depend on your purpose for the move, the length of your stay, and the regulations of the country you're moving to. Complete the application forms truthfully; inaccurate data can delay or prevent you from getting a visa. Some governments will require supporting documents. You might need to prove that you have the financial means to stay in the country, a job, or acceptance to an institute or school. You might be asked to provide biometric data such as fingerprints or iris scans to be used as ID.

Some countries have simple visa requirements, and others have very complex prerequisites. It's up to you to do the research required to obtain the correct visa.

Visas do have expiration dates, which vary by country. Visit the website for the consulate of the country you are moving to or visit the consulate in person for more detailed information on visas.

You should also enroll in STEP, which is the acronym for the Smart Traveler Enrollment Program. Registering for STEP allows you to receive information pertaining to safety conditions in the country you're going to and allows the US embassy to reach out to you in case of emergency.

Some countries require a list of all vaccinations you've received, and they may require or encourage you to get more. Check the medical services and the medical system of your designated country, because some require that you be responsible for all medical costs. Make sure that you have copies of your prescriptions so the doctor you find in your new country can order them.

While you are researching normal issues like where to live and the cost of living in that area, take some time to familiarize yourself with at least some of the language. You may not be fluent by the time you're ready to move, but having a basic communicative understanding of phrases and places will be a tremendous help. Knowing some of the language will help you make friends with your new neighbors.

Children

Traveling to a foreign land with children can be both an exciting adventure and a daunting adjustment for the young ones. They are leaving everything they are comfortable with behind—and in some cases, that includes their language. The loss of friends and security may be overwhelming to them.

It falls on the parent to try to create a positive experience for the children. Prioritize their needs over yours. Include them in the research you do on the history and culture of the country. Find places you want to visit together, and take time to study and practice the language together. Discover how your child's interests can be applied in the new country. Promote the expression of their feelings and listen to what they are saying, not just verbally but also through their actions and reactions.

Do your best to supply the stability that the children may feel is slipping away with the move. They will miss their friends. Assure them that those feelings are normal and that they can text, write, and call to stay in contact, while you also encourage them to make new friends.

And most important is the attitude that you project. Your approach to the move will greatly influence their positive or negative response. You can spark their curiosity and sense of adventure while helping them feel safe in the new environment. And there is nothing more supportive than a hug and an expression of your love.

Your Well-Being

An international move is difficult. In many instances you will be leaving family and friends behind, which is emotionally stressful. You will be walking into a new environment with distinctive customs, language barriers, and cultural differences. Unless your employer is helping you move, you likely won't have a strong support system when you arrive. It can be much easier on you, and your family, if you enter this new adventure knowing that you are not alone and that you have cultivated a new support group for yourself.

To avoid a sense of isolation once you've arrived, check online to see if there are other immigrants or expats you can communicate with before the move. Online forums allow you to familiarize yourself with the customs and lifestyles you'll soon be experiencing. It's a great way to meet people who can provide advice and guidance for the changes coming to your life.

While you are going through the lengthy process of pre-move requisites, be certain to take time for yourself. Find ways to express your excitement and your reservations about the move, whether it is to a partner, to a friend, or to your personal journal. Don't bottle things up.

Pack a small first-aid kit so that you have items handy that you are familiar with, like anti-diarrheal medication, headache relievers, packaged electrolytes, and something for stomach distress. Introducing new foods and the stress of such a major move can be rough on the system, and these items might be difficult to find in your new country when you're unfamiliar with the language or the brands available.

Maintain your normal healthy diet, exercise schedule, and sleep habits to ensure that you are fully functional mentally and physically. The decision to move and the first step of applying for proper documentation are just the beginning of what lies ahead of you.

Know the Laws

If you are driving across borders, know the laws of that country. This is true even if you are driving from the continental US through Canada to Alaska. It is your responsibility to know what is permissible and what is not. The biggest problem when crossing the US border into Canada or Mexico is the possession of firearms.

According to the Canada Border Services Agency, a non-Canadian may import firearms into Canada for a valid purpose. Valid purposes can include (but are not limited to) the following:

- Hunting during hunting season (limited to nonrestricted firearms only)

- Use in competitions
- Repair
- In-transit movement, i.e., moving in the most direct route possible from point A to point B, through Canada
- Protection against wildlife in remote areas (limited to non-restricted firearms only)[21]

Certain firearms are prohibited, and the proper documentation and a fee must accompany any that are allowed. The owner of the firearm will need to obtain a Canadian Firearm License.

In Mexico you must have a permit from the Secretariat of National Defense. These cannot be issued at the border and must be obtained before attempting to enter the country.

Gun laws are very different in Canada and Mexico, and probably in every other destination country too. If you are relocating with a firearm, research the laws of any country whose border you cross as well as the laws in your final locality.

How Do You Get Your Stuff There?

What should you move to the new country? What should you keep in storage? How long will you be gone? Is the move for work, school, or just a change of pace? All of these are major considerations.

There are international movers who will handle everything for you, which is ideal if you're moving for business reasons. They begin with a consultation and take it from there. They can guide you through pre-move planning, packing your items, transporting them, tracking them, and scheduling the delivery. They help with all aspects of logistics, including compiling the necessary personal information and paperwork for the new country and managing the customs clearances needed to receive your goods when they arrive. International moving companies do their best to accommodate your personal specifications and needs.

Some people want to move independently, but a self-move out of the country is a tremendous amount of work, can be very tricky, and—as Devra found out—is extremely expensive. In the early '80s, she had to find creative ways to get her stuff from here to there with the least amount of money.

My husband was a low-ranking military guy who received orders for deployment to South Korea. His rank meant that the US government wouldn't cover the cost for me to move with him. If I wanted to be near him, I had to foot the bill on my own.

It seemed like everything I could take was limited. I had to fit all my belongings in a suitcase that would be accepted by the airline. My two-year-old daughter's toys and things that I knew would be important for her filled the other suitcase. The strict limit imposed by the airline was two suitcases.

I did some research and found out that because of my husband's rank, I would not be able to shop in the base post exchange (PX) unless I had a job on base, which wouldn't happen immediately. Things that we consider staples, like coffee makers and filters, weren't available to me through the PX at reasonable prices.

After checking out a variety of options, I decided to box up a lot of what we would need, including a healthy supply of toddler food, and mail the boxes to my husband's base address. I hoped they wouldn't be lost in the mail or flagged by customs. The US postal service was much less expensive than UPS or FedEx for military personnel, so I went with US mail. It worked out perfectly. For a very low price I could send everything by ground, which really meant that it traveled by ship—the cheapest yet slowest method available.

My one suitcase held enough to provide for us until all the boxes arrived. Within three weeks, everything else I'd shipped—everything I thought I'd need—arrived in South Korea. That was great, but there were things that I had never imagined I would need when I arrived in this new country.

The village I had moved to was just outside the demilitarized zone and very primitive compared to my home in the United States. In the '80s, local Korean stores did not sell disposable diapers. When you have a two-year-old and no running water in the apartment, disposable diapers are an absolute must. I was living a nightmare. To wash cloth diapers, I had to go outside to the pump with a bucket, fill the bucket with water, heat the water, and so on. A week after we arrived, I was potty training a two-year-old out of necessity. Neither of us was ready for this.

It's very easy to imagine that in another country they will have all the same things that the US would offer, until you get there and find out that's not always true.

The other major lesson of this move was to learn at least the basics of the language before you move to a foreign country. How arrogant I was in hindsight that I thought everyone in the world speaks English (or, I wasn't thinking). The simplest of tasks, like asking for directions to get to my job for my first day at work or buying food at the local market, were impossible. It didn't take me long to realize I should have learned some basic Korean before I made this journey.

The hardest part of my international move to Korea in 1984 was that I did not plan well for my return to the States. I purchased beautiful furniture while I was living abroad, which I had to leave behind. I had estimated costs based on my budget to move to the country but hadn't factored in the cost of the move back to the States. It was not just the extremely high shipping costs for large heavy items but the fact that there were very few companies equipped for international shipping at that time. I was told it could take six months for someone to pick up my living room set, and I was leaving in thirty days. It was an epic fail on my part that meant the loss of my hand-carved, beautiful furniture. Fortunately, times have changed, and there are many companies offering international shipping now.

DEVRA'S TIP Solid research can prevent a future disaster and a lot of stress. It takes time to research and explore possibilities, but it is well worth it.

The resources section of this book provides links that may assist you in completing a successful international move.

Conclusion

A primary characteristic for a happy move of any kind is a healthy mindset that views the transition as an adventure, a fresh start that will bring new experiences, new friendships, and an expansion of your life knowledge.

Devra shares:

> The best thing about moving as much as I have is that every place is different, alive with its own culture and experiences. The tastes, the smells, and the ambiance are all unique. From the arid Southwest to the beaches of the coasts to the country style of the South, each new location had its own beauty and wonders to share. I grew as a person from every place I called home.

If you follow the guidelines laid out in this book, learn from the experiences shared, and approach the move with an open mind and open heart, moving can be stress-free and rewarding. A bright, fulfilling future can be the end result of your happy move.

Acknowledgments

Our appreciation goes out to Dr. Donna Marks, Rebecca Stinson, Brett Nilsson, and Celeste Hoehne; each one contributed in their very special way.

We wish to acknowledge Jeff Lockridge, Manager of Media and Public Relations for U-Haul®, as well as Terrie Duren, Business Marketing Manager, and James L. Burati III, Chief Sales Officer, both of 1-800-PACK-RAT—they are all truly dedicated to the act of moving people and were of assistance to the authors by providing information and images for this book.

And a special thanks to Richard and Michele for encouraging Devra to share her experiences and the knowledge she gained through so many moves.

Appendix: Resources

Before You Move

Verifying a Company's Legitimacy

Better Business Bureau, bbb.org
Find a local BBB office directory, bbb.org/bbb-directory

Landlord and Tenant Laws by State

Alabama

   alarise.org/wp-content/uploads/2015/08/The-Alabama-Tenants
      -Handbook-4.22.2020.pdf
   https://www.alarise.org/resources/the-alabama-tenants-handbook/

Alaska

   law.alaska.gov/pdf/consumer/LandlordTenant_web.pdf

Arizona

   housing.az.gov/general-public/landlord-and-tenant-act

Arkansas

   arkansasag.gov/consumer-protection/home/landlord-and
      -tenant-rights/

California

   courts.ca.gov/documents/California-Tenants-Guide.pdf

Colorado

   leg.colorado.gov/sites/default/files/images/olls/crs2020-title-38.pdf

Connecticut

   jud.ct.gov/publications/hm031.pdf

Delaware

   delcode.delaware.gov/title25/c053/index.html

District of Columbia

ota.dc.gov/sites/default/files/dc/sites/ota/publication/attachments
/2015%2007%2003%20OTA%20DC%20Tenant%20Bill%20
of%20Rights%20ODAI-OTA%20FINAL.pdf

Florida

fdacs.gov/Consumer-Resources/Landlord-Tenant-Law-in-Florida

Georgia

dca.ga.gov/node/2945

Hawaii

cca.hawaii.gov/ocp/files/2022/06/2022-Landlord-Tenant
-Handbook-003.pdf
https://cca.hawaii.gov/ocp/landlord-tenant/

Idaho

ag.idaho.gov/content/uploads/2018/04/LandlordTenant.pdf

Illinois

illinoisattorneygeneral.gov/consumers/landlordtenantrights0404.pdf

Indiana

in.gov/health/eph/files/Tenants_Rights_doc.pdf

Iowa

legis.iowa.gov/docs/Legis_Guide/2013/LGLSL004.PDF

Kansas

hcci-ks.org/wp-content/uploads/2014/12/Kansastenantshandbook
2007.pdf

Kentucky

apps.legislature.ky.gov/law/statutes/chapter.aspx?id=39159

Louisiana

ag.state.la.us/Files/Article/10/Documents/AGuidetoLALandlord
TenantLaws.pdf

Maine
  legislature.maine.gov/lawlibrary/what-is-maines-law-on-landlord
   -tenant-issues/9477

Maryland
  marylandattorneygeneral.gov/Pages/CPD/landlords.aspx
  https://www.marylandattorneygeneral.gov/CPD%20Documents
   /Tips-Publications/landlordTenantPDF.pdf

Massachusetts
  mass.gov/guides/the-attorney-generals-guide-to-landlord-and
   -tenant-rights

Michigan
  legislature.mi.gov/Publications/tenantlandlord.pdf

Minnesota
  ag.state.mn.us/consumer/handbooks/lt/default.asp

Mississippi
  msbar.org/for-the-public/consumer-information/cur-rent-law
   -for-tenants-and-landlords/

Missouri
  ago.mo.gov/docs/default-source/publications/landlord-tenantlaw.pdf

Montana
  dojmt.gov/consumer/tenants-and-landlords/

Nebraska
  nrec.nebraska.gov/legal/landlordacttoc.html

Nevada
  leg.state.nv.us/nrs/nrs-118a.html

New Hampshire
  doj.nh.gov/consumer/sourcebook/renting.htm

New Jersey

nj.gov/dca/divisions/codes/offices/landlord_tenant_information
.html

New Mexico

rld.state.nm.us/uploads/files/00%202019%20NM%20
UORRA%20-%20CHAPTER%2047%20-%20for%20web%20
publication.pdf

New York

ag.ny.gov/sites/default/files/tenants_rights.pdf

North Carolina

files.nc.gov/ncdhhs/documents/files/hcbs/landlord
_tenant_brochure.pdf

North Dakota

attorneygeneral.nd.gov/consumer-resources/tenant-rights

Ohio

codes.ohio.gov/ohio-revised-code/chapter-5321

Oklahoma

oksenate.gov/sites/default/files/2019-12/os41.pdf

Oregon

osbar.org/public/legalinfo/landlordtenant.html

Pennsylvania

legis.state.pa.us/WU01/LI/LI/US/PDF/1951/0/0020..PDF

Rhode Island

courts.ri.gov/Courts/districtcourt/PDF/Handbook.pdf

South Carolina

scstatehouse.gov/code/t27c040.php

South Dakota
consumer.sd.gov/fastfacts/landlordtenant.aspx

Tennessee
tncourts.gov/sites/default/files/docs/general_sessions_cases
_handout.pdf

Texas
texasattorneygeneral.gov/consumer-protection/home-real-estate
-and-travel/renters-rights

Utah
le.utah.gov/xcode/title57/chapter22/C57-22_1800010118000101
.pdf

Vermont
cvoeo.org/client_media/files/HAP/VTT_Definitive_Guide_and
_Illustrated_Guide.pdf

Virginia
dhcd.virginia.gov/sites/default/files/Docx/landlord-tenant/2019
-landlord-tenant-handbook.pdf

Washington
commerce.wa.gov/wp-content/uploads/2016/12/2012-Landlord
-Tenant-WA-AG.pdf

West Virginia
ago.wv.gov/consumerprotection/documents/renters%27%20
rights%20brochure.pdf

Wisconsin
datcp.wi.gov/Documents/LT-LandlordTenantGuide497.pdf

Wyoming
equaljustice.wy.gov/application/files/6715/7894/2198/Renters
_Rights_Handout.pdf

Background on Neighborhoods

AreaVibes, areavibes.com

MyMove, mymove.com/moving/planning/how-safe-is-my
-neighborhood

Nextdoor, nextdoor.com

SpotCrime, spotcrime.com

Sex Offender Public Registry

Dru Sjodin National Sex Offender Public Website, nsopw.gov

States Not Listed in National Sex Offender Public Registry

Arkansas

ark.org/offender-search/index.php

Illinois

isp.illinois.gov/Sor/Disclaimer

Minnesota

minnesota.staterecords.org/sexoffender

New Hampshire

weare.nh.gov/weare-police-department/safety/pages/
state-of-new-hampshire-sex-offender-registry

New York

ny.gov/services/search-sex-offender-registry

Oregon

sexoffenders.oregon.gov/ConditionsOfUse

Texas

publicsite.dps.texas.gov/SexOffenderRegistry

West Virginia

westvirginia.staterecords.org/sexoffender

Vermont

vcic.vermont.gov/sor

Finding Your Home

Apartments.com, apartments.com

Realtor.com, www.realtor.com

RentCafe, www.rentcafe.com

Trulia, trulia.com

Zillow, zillow.com

Considering the Weather

AccuWeather, accuweather.com

Weather.com, weather.com

Camping/RV Plans

Go Camping America, gocampingamerica.com

Go RVing, gorving.com

RV Camping, rv-camping.org

Who to Notify

Official USPS® Change-of-Address, moversguide.usps.com/mgo
/disclaimer

Preparing to Move

Self-Move Rental Truck Companies

Penske Truck Rental, pensketruckrental.com

U-Haul®, uhaul.com

U-Haul Truck Share 24/7®, uhaul.com/videos/Trucks-Videos
/Truck-Share

Fuel Locations and Prices

AAA, aaa.com/travelinfo/gas-prices.htm

GasBuddy, gasbuddy.com

Container Moving Companies

1-800-PACK-RAT | Zippy Shell, 1800packrat.com/resources
/partners/key-partners/zippy-shell
U-Haul® U-Box®, uhaul.com/UBox
UPack®, upack.com

Traditional Moving Companies and Long-Distance Movers

Allegiance offers senior citizen and military discounts and provides
piano, antique, and grandfather clock specialists, www.allegiance
-relocation.com

Allied Van Lines is good for both domestic and international moves,
allied.com

American Van Lines are rated as friendly with trustworthy staff,
americanvanlines.com

Nationwide Moving Services offers a 10-percent-off discount for verified first responders and military members, nwmoving.com

New Leaf Moving Group donates to St. Jude Children's Research
Hospital, newleafmovinggroup.com

North American Moving Services also has storage and unpacking
services, northamerican.com

Safe Ship Moving Services provides veteran-owned and family-
operated long-distance relocation services, safeshipmoves.com

Simple Path Moving is best for interstate moving, mysimplepaths
.com

Trinity Relocation offers group discounts available for AARP, AAA, military, and students, trinity-relocation.com

Two Men and a Truck, twomenandatruck.com

United Van Lines, unitedvanlines.com

FMCSA and USDOT Licenses

Federal Motor Carrier Safety Association (FMCSA) and the United States Department of Transportation (USDOT), fmcsa.dot.gov

Moving with Pets

Animal and Plant Health Inspection Service, aphis.usda.gov/aphis/pet-travel

Guam quarantine rules, amcguam.com/moving-to-guam-with-pets

Hawaii quarantine rules, hdoa.hawaii.gov/ai/aqs/aqs-info

International Pet and Animal Transportation Association, ipata.org/find-ipata-pet-shippers

MyMove, mymove.com/moving/kids-and-pets/moving-with-pets

Traveling with pets, cdc.gov/importation/traveling-with-pets.html

US Department of Transportation, service animals, transportation.gov/individuals/aviation-consumer-protection/service-animals

Time for the Physical Work

Packing Tips

AHappyMove.com/videos

Plants

US Department of Agriculture, Animal and Plant Health Inspection Service, aphis.usda.gov/aphis/ourfocus/planthealth

Firearms

Firearms Owners' Protection Act, congress.gov/bill/99th-congress/senate-bill/49

During the Move

Attractions

National recreation areas, usparkpass.com/map-of-national-parks
State parks, stateparks.com/index.html
US unusual attractions, atlasobscura.com/things-to-do/united-states

After the Move

Unloading

Hire a Helper, hireahelper.com
Moving Help®, uhaul.com/MovingHelp

Other Moves

Military Moves

Do-it-yourself military moves, 1800packrat.com/move-my-stuff/military-moving

Military.com helps answer questions for the military family, military.com

Military OneSource offers resources for permanent change of station and other military moves, militaryonesource.mil/moving-housing /moving/pcs-and-military-moves

Military OneSource also provides a helpful tool to search for military installations according to your desired criteria, installations.military onesource.mil/?looking-for-a=program/program-service=2/focus =program

Military Moves with Pets

Animal and Plant Health Inspection Service, aphis.usda.gov/aphis /pet-travel

Air Mobility Command, amc.af.mil/AMC-Travel-Site/AMC-Pet -Travel-Page

Dogs on Deployment is a nonprofit that offers care for dogs of military personnel during deployment, dogsondeployment.org

Military One Source, militaryonesource.mil/moving-housing /moving/planning-your-move/moving-with-pets

International Moves

Country information, travel.state.gov/content/travel/en/international -travel/International-Travel-Country-Information-Pages.html

Guide to living abroad from Expat.com, expat.com/en/guide

Gun control in Mexico, mexlaw.com/some-basic-facts-about-gun -control-in-mexico-2

How to move out of the US, internationalliving.com/how-to-move -out-of-the-u-s

Importing firearms into Canada, cbsa-asfc.gc.ca/import/iefw-iefa -eng.html

Meeting people and learning about other cultures, meetup.com

Tips for becoming an expat from the International Citizens Group, internationalcitizens.com/expatriates/five-tips-for-becoming-an -expat.php

Tips for planning an international move, wickedgoodtraveltips.com /2022/03/04/guide-to-planning-an-international-move-key-things -to-know

Travel advisories, travel.state.gov/content/travel/en/traveladvisories /traveladvisories.html

Notes

1. Better Business Bureau, "BBB Scam Alert: Avoid Moving Scams This National Moving Month," May 2, 2022, https://www.bbb .org/article/scams/24198-bbb-scam-alert-avoid-moving-scams -this-national-moving-month.
2. Brandon, "When Is Peak Moving Season? [2023]," MovingLabor .com, last updated November 11, 2022, https://www.moving labor.com/blog/when-is-peak-moving-season.
3. Jeff Lockridge (Manager of Media and Public Relations, U-Haul®), interview with the authors, August 2, 2022.
4. Nancy Cooper, ed., "America's Best Customer Service 2020," Newsweek, https://www.newsweek.com/americas-best-customer -service-2020/services-transportation-travel.
5. Lockridge, interview.
6. Lockridge, interview.
7. Lockridge, interview.
8. James L. Burati III (Chief Sales Officer, 1-800-PACK-RAT/ Zippy Shell), interview with the authors, July 26, 2022.
9. Lockridge, interview.
10. Crimes and Criminal Procedure 2011, 18 U.S.C. § 922 (2022), https://uscode.house.gov/view.xhtml?req=%28title%3A18 +section%3A922+edition%3Aprelim%29.
11. Code of Federal Regulations 2020, 27 § 478 (2020), https:// www.govinfo.gov/content/pkg/CFR-2021-title27-vol3/pdf /CFR-2021-title27-vol3.pdf.
12. Firearm Owners' Protection Act of 1986, Pub. L. No. 99-308, 100 Stat. 449 (1986), https://www.govinfo.gov/app/details /STATUTE-100/STATUTE-100-Pg449/summary.

13. Rebecca Stinson, discussion with the authors, July 2022.

14. Brett Nilsson, discussion with the authors, July 2022.

15. Military OneSource, "PCs Entitlements," US Department of Defense, June 17, 2022, https://www.militaryonesource.mil /moving-housing/moving/planning-your-move/military-pcs -entitlements/.

16. Burati, interview.

17. Burati, interview.

18. Burati, interview.

19. Dr. Donna Marks, discussion with the authors, August 2022.

20. U.S. Department of State, "Consular Affairs by the Numbers," updated January 2020, https://travel.state.gov/content/dam /travel/CA-By-the-Number-2020.pdf.

21. "Import and export a firearm or weapon into Canada," Canada Border Services Agency, accessed November 8, 2022, https:// www.cbsa-asfc.gc.ca/import/iefw-iefa-eng.html.

About the Authors

The Mover—Devra Jacobs

With twenty-nine moves under her belt, Devra is an authority on moving. She and her family have moved all over the USA and even relocated once to Korea.

Along the way, Devra has learned numerous valuable do-it-yourself lessons on everything from how to pack properly to how to hire the right movers for cross-country moves. In these pages, she shares the good, the bad, and the happy experiences that can help you have *A Happy Move*.

The owner of Dancing Word Group, Devra is a successful literary agent, representing both mainstream and higher-consciousness authors.

The Writer—Brit Elders

An internationally published author, Brit focuses her research and work on nonfiction topics. She has written books, articles, documentary films, and ghostwritten and edited for others with the goal of learning something new from each project.

She is the CEO of ShirleyMacLaine.com, a position she's held since its inception. An advocate for naturopathic health and healthy eating, Brit has hosted radio programs and been a guest on radio and television in the US as well as other countries.

Brit has lived in Arizona her entire life.

For more information on moving, visit AHappyMove.com.

Your Lists